Library of
Davidson College

18th CENTURY SYMPHONIES

ENCORE MUSIC EDITIONS
Reprints of outstanding works on music

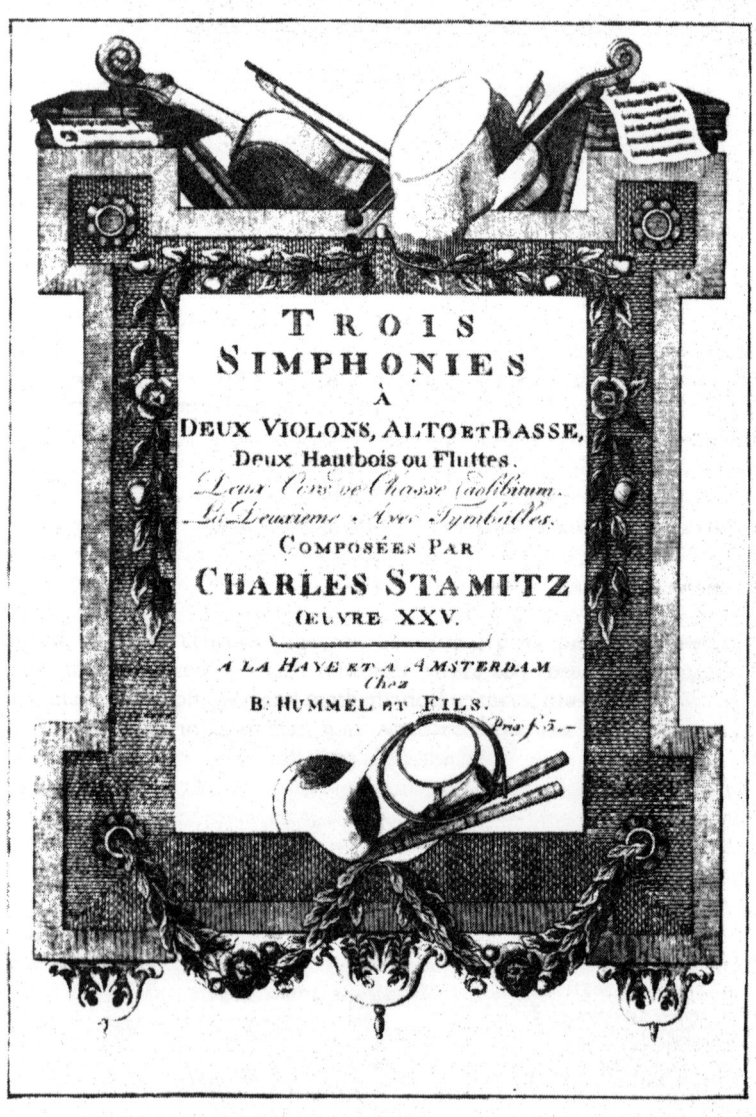

Cover of an 18th century set of orchestral parts

18th CENTURY SYMPHONIES

A short history of the Symphony in the 18th century with special reference to the works in the two Series

Early Classical Symphonies

and

18th Century Overtures

by

ADAM CARSE

(Fellow of the Royal Academy of Music)

HYPERION PRESS, INC.
Westport, Connecticut

Published in 1951 by Augener Ltd., London
Hyperion reprint edition 1979
Library of Congress Catalog Number 78-66900
ISBN 0-88355-731-2
Printed in the United States of America

Library of Congress Cataloging in Publication Data
Carse, Adam von Ahn, 1878-1958.
  18th century symphonies.

  (Encore music editions)
  Reprint of the 1951 ed. published by Augener, London
Includes index.
  1. Symphony. I. Title.
[ML1255.C3 1979]   785.1'1'09033   78-66900
ISBN 0-88355-731-2

Contents

		page
I.	Introduction	1
II.	The French *Ouverture* and the Italian *Sinfonia*	8
III.	The independent concert-symphony	14
IV.	The form of the movements	28
V.	Score, parts and orchestration	40
VI.	Analysis of the form of the movements in the two series *Early Classical Symphonies* and *18th Century Overtures*.	51
VII.	Conclusion	60
Appendix A.	Composers of symphonies or overtures published in the 18th century.	72
Appendix B.	Some Composers of unpublished symphonies	74
Index		75

Abbreviations

E.C.S. = Early Classical Symphonies, edited and/or arranged by Adam Carse *(Augener Ltd.)*

18th C. O. = 18th Century Overtures, edited and/or arranged by Adam Carse *(Augener Ltd.)*

G A. = *Gesamtausgabe*, Complete Collected works of Haydn and Mozart *(Breitkopf & Härtel)*.

D.D.T. = *Denkmäler Deutscher Tonkunst*.

Definitions

Basso continuo. The bass part in general, but in particular the bass part to which the requisite harmony was added on a a keyboard or chordal instrument, sometimes provided with figures which define the chords.

Coda. A Tail-piece, ending, refrain or epilogue, at the end of an Exposition or at the end of a movement.

Development. The middle portion of a movement in Sonata Form, between the Exposition and the Recapitulation, in which the thematic matter is treated in various ways and in various keys.

Episode. A theme or matter which occurs only once.

Exposition. The first part of a movement in Sonata Form, embracing the First Subject, transition, Second Subject and Coda (if any). In a Fugue, the first statements of the subject and answer by each part in turn.

Recapitulation. The third and last part of a movement in Sonata Form, following the Development, in which the First and Second Subjects are re-stated, both in the tonic key, with the final Coda (if any).

Semi-Sonata Form. Not a recognised term, but used here for movements in Sonata Form in which the First Subject is not re-stated when the original key returns after the development.

Tonality. Key, key-relationship.

Transition. Change of key or modulation; applied to that portion of a Sonata or Symphony which follows the First Subject and leads into the key in which the Second Subject is to be stated. Usually a *Tutti* in the old symphonies.

Tutti. Altogether; a passage in which all instruments take part, usually *forte* in the old symphonies.

I

INTRODUCTION

IN Haydn's last twelve and Mozart's last three, may be found the culmination of its growth, but not the history of the symphony in the 18th century. The story of the symphony reaches back at least to the French *Ouverture* and the Italian *Sinfonia*, both of which took shape during the second half of the 17th century; it traverses rather than follows the path trodden by Bach and Handel; it runs through and survives, even welcomes, a change in the style and texture of musical composition that was already in progress before the middle of the 18th century, and after having been nourished and stabilized by a copious output of works in the 'fifties, 'sixties and 'seventies, reaches its apogee in the 'eighties and 'nineties of that century. But although Haydn and Mozart were the only two composers who were able to take full advantage of all that had accrued to the symphony during the earlier stages of its growth, the credit for having nursed it and seen it through its youthful troubles must go to a large number of composers whose works are now almost entirely forgotten, and many of whose names are barely remembered.

It is now many years since the present writer, while pursuing investigations into the history of orchestration, came into close touch with a vast quantity of music which lay undisturbed in many a library in the form of printed orchestral parts of symphonies and overtures, usually in little sets of eight parts, by composers, some of whose names were more or less familiar, and some of which were quite strange. None of these works ever appeared in concert programmes, musical histories ignored them, and when any of them were offered in the catalogues of second-hand music dealers, they were inexpensive and generally remained unsold. Further search and experience revealed ever more and more of these printed parts, but never a single score; all were 18th century publications, most of them from the second half of the century, and the eight parts were commonly for a standard combination, namely, four parts for the string orchestra, and two each for oboes and horns.

This great mass of forgotten music constitutes, so to speak, the contents of the workshop in which the symphony was made; it represents the experience that was accumulating and was destined to be summed up and transcended in the few 18th century symphonies that are now heard in our concert-halls, namely, the last few and best of those composed by Haydn and Mozart.

The works constituting this immense storehouse of neglected music could not be performed because the necessary material for so doing was lacking; in other words, it could not be bought. At that time—about forty years ago—a few of those forgotten symphonies were being issued in the great series *Denkmäler Deutscher Tonkunst;* but they were all printed in score, and the separate parts that are indispensable for a performance by an orchestra were not to be had. From about 1922 a number of similar works were being published in score, "*herausgegeben und gearbeitet*," by Dr. Robert Sondheimer, and a few isolated works have since made their appearance in modern print; nevertheless, the conductor who wished to perform an 18th century symphony by any composer other than Haydn or Mozart would have found his choice severely limited, and in most cases the parts would have to be copied by hand before the work could be played.

The idea of presenting some of these symphonies in a form suitable for performance under present-day conditions had occurred to the writer soon after he had come into contact with this great cemetery of forgotten music. If not one of the symphonies was a masterpiece, there were plenty of them that would make quite pleasant hearing, and all had some historical significance in that they revealed the process by which the symphony had been evolved. Moreover, they were short, only a small orchestra was required, and they were technically fairly easy to play and were therefore very suitable for performance by amateur and school orchestras.

The idea did not bear fruit until 1935, when with the co-operation of Augener Ltd., a series entitled EARLY CLASSICAL

SYMPHONIES was launched, edited and arranged (when necessary) by the writer, in which each work was made available both in score and in parts, and was offered at a moderate price. This series has now reached its twelfth number, and a somewhat similar series, entitled 18TH CENTURY OVERTURES, begun in 1939, now contains seven numbers.

The choice of the works in both series has been governed largely by selection, but partly by chance. No one person could ever hope to acquire a complete knowledge of so many hundreds of works scattered about in dozens of libraries, some of them barely accessible and uncatalogued, more especially as all the works appeared in a form which required transcription into score before the music could be fairly judged. It must therefore have been chance that has brought some of these works into the hands of the writer and that has kept others out of his reach.

In selecting a work to represent a particular composer, one is naturally inclined to choose the best that can be found. Experience has shown, however, that in the case of these 18th century symphonies, it is hardly ever possible to find one that is better than its fellows throughout all the three or four movements. One with a good first movement may have a weak slow movement, or a charming slow movement may be flanked by inferior first and last movements. The selection, therefore, should not be regarded as a series of picked works, each the best that its composer could offer; on the other hand, each work is no more than an average specimen, no better or worse than its fellows, but all are typical of the general standard which prevailed amongst composers of a large class who were endowed with varying natural gifts, but to all of whom was denied the supreme gift that reveals itself only in the mature works of Haydn and Mozart.

Nevertheless, no standard has yet been found by means of which the intrinsic value of a piece of music can be measured, or one which will infallibly distinguish between the work of the greater and the lesser man. Taking their work as a whole, it is easy enough to see that one composer wrote better music than another; it is easy to see that Haydn's symphonies are better than Vanhall's, or that Mozart's are far superior to Dittersdorf's. But when put to the test, as it often is when the authenticity of a particular work is in question, the process seems invariably to break down, and even experts are unable to distinguish between the first-class and the second-rate article. When Mandyczewski, the editor of the complete (as yet uncompleted) symphonies of Haydn, had collected all the symphonies extant that bore Haydn's name, he found that in addition to the 104 authenticated works, there were some 74 that were not accounted for in Haydn's own catalogue of his symphonies;[1] of these, 38 were found in print under other composers' names, and were therefore classed as spurious, but 36 remained, and still remain, works of uncertain parentage, and until some conclusive evidence, other than their musical quality, is found, the authenticity of these symphonies will always be open to question.[2]

At least two of the symphonies that appeared in the Complete works of Mozart have since been proved to have been written by other composers.[3] It is obvious that the style and quality of a piece of music does not provide conclusive evidence that it was written by one particular composer, and that no boundary line can be set up which will clearly distinguish between the work of the great and the lesser man.

This book is an attempt to show how the symphony developed during the 18th century, with particular reference to the scores that are now easily accessible in the two series EARLY CLASSICAL SYMPHONIES and 18TH CENTURY OVERTURES. These, of course, can be usefully supplemented by the scores available in the *Denkmäler* series,[4] the Sondheimer series,[5] and by any others that may be found.

It should be understood, however, that the author's purpose is to show how the symphony developed rather than to show what it had become by the end of the century; the emphasis is on the process of growth rather than on the result of the growth. The reader who hopes to find in these pages a critical analysis and full appreciation of the last few and best symphonies of Haydn and Mozart will be disappointed. That ground has already been well covered in books, essays, articles, and in countless analytical programme notes; moreover, these works are familiar; they are constantly played at concerts, they are heard by radio transmission over and over

---
[1] Elssler's *Haydn-Verzeichnis*. [2] K 18 and K 444, by C. F. Abel and Michael Haydn.
[3] Some of these have since been identified, but many more have in the meantime been added to the list of those classed as "doubtful." (Larsen, *Drei Haydn Kataloge*.)
[4] Not now easily obtainable, and very expensive.   [5] Bernoulli Ed., Berlin.

18th CENTURY SYMPHONIES 5

again in the course of every year, the gramophone will repeat them as often as is required, and all of them can be studied in miniature scores.

On all the works for which the present writer is responsible the words " edited and/or arranged " will be found, and this calls for some explanation.

Whether it survives in MS or in print, if it is to be adequately performed under present-day conditions, all 18th century orchestral music requires editing. Most of the overtures and symphonies have been handed down in no other form than in parts, and these parts are usually well sprinkled with copyist's or engraver's errors, sometimes with both. Many of the printed works passed from one publisher to another without reference to the composer, without his permission, and without any payment to him. In fact, it is practically certain that most if not all of the republished works were taken gratuitously, without either permission or payment. Except in the few cases when the composer dealt directly with the first publisher, the composer never saw any proofs and was not given any opportunity of seeing that his work was correctly printed. The dynamic signs and marks of expression (if there are any!) are usually carelessly and inconsistently indicated; the slurring, even in the original sources, is sketchy, haphazard, and often ambiguous; the slur may be used to indicate phrasing, articulation, bowing, or nothing in particular except *legato*. These things and many other details must be reduced to some sort of order by an editor, and such conveniences as rehearsal letters and good turns-over must be provided. It is only those who have never come into close touch with the sources of 18th century music that resent the intermediation of the editor.

Arranging, by which we understand some rearrangement of the notes actually written by the composer, is quite another matter, and one which may or may not be necessary. All the works in question belong to the period during which the so-called conductor sat at the harpsichord or piano and played the *basso-continuo* with its requisite harmony. Until fairly late in the 18th century the composer did not usually lay out his string parts in such a way that a complete and balanced harmony was assured; it was left to the conductor at the keyboard instrument to complete the chords and give to the music the harmonic background which was only partially or vaguely suggested in the orchestral parts. Moreover, composers were apt to think in three parts, and inclined to write the two violin parts close together and separated by a yawning gulf from the bass part, just as they did in sonatas for two violins and bass, and also in the orchestral trios that were much favoured by Johann Stamitz and his disciples. The viola part is usually little more than a duplication of the bass part at the octave above, and at its best gets only the harmonic leavings of the violin parts. Sometimes they did not even trouble to write three parts.[1] An easy and quick way of creating a second violin part was to write " col primo " on the stave, just as a viola part was quickly made by scribbling " col basso." The music then becomes all top and bottom, with nothing in the middle except what the keyboard and two or three wind instruments might provide. It should not be supposed that this duplication of parts was done in order to reinforce or intensify the two outer parts; neither of these required reinforcement; it was just a labour-saving habit, a quick way of getting over the ground, and one which was much practiced at a time when composers wrote a great quantity of music for immediate use, and were obliged to get it done as quickly as possible.

For use under present conditions, when there is no conductor at the piano, and when there is a hiatus in the centre of the orchestral lay-out, some rearrangement of the inner string parts is necessary *unless the music is to be misrepresented*, and this usually takes the form of a re-lay-out of the second violin and viola parts. But this does not, and should not, add any fresh matter to the music, nor any fresh colour, nor does it modernize the style; it merely supplies on the inner strings the harmony which was formerly supplied by the " conductor " on a keyboard-instrument. The purist, of course, will protest against this " unwarranted interference with the text of the composer," and will no doubt prefer to *misrepresent* the music by playing it in bare outline, as a mere skeleton, without it proper complement of harmony, the harmony which the composer meant it to have even though he didn't write it all out in the score.

---

[1] Bu y composers sometimes wrote only the treble and bass, and left it to an assistant to fill n the rest

Not all 18th century composers were possessed of an immaculate technique, and they sometimes bungled their part-writing, either from lack of skill or from more carelessness or haste. Some of the obviously clumsy mistakes may well be ironed out in an arrangement. Such carelessness as allowing the bass part, when played an octave higher by the viola, to rise above the melody part[1] is by no means uncommon, and when the oboes are directed to play "col violini," care is not always taken to see that their downward compass is not exceeded. These things were done inadvertently, and are typical of the casual and hasty manner in which much 18th century music was written. The readjustment of such blunders need not trouble the conscience of any arranger.

The foregoing will explain the words "edited and/or arranged," and will at the same time make it clear that the scores in question should not be regarded as historical reprints; a performing edition of an old work is never a historical document—the two cannot be combined and should not be confused.

In the following pages the story begins with an examination of overtures or symphonies that were originally instrumental introductions to operas or other works, and which then without any change were used as concert-music.

Similar works written on exactly the same lines, but independently of any dramatic works, and their subsequent structural enlargement due to the growth of Sonata Form, then come under consideration, and the process by which the concert-symphony outgrew and eventually detached itself from the opera-overture is followed up to the point where the two types became clearly distinguishable both as regards their form and purpose. The form of the movements is treated separately, also the orchestration, and an analysis of the form of each movement of the works included in the two series EARLY CLASSICAL SYMPHONIES and 18TH CENTURY OVERTURES leads to some concluding remarks in which, as has already been pointed out, there is no attempt to survey in detail the final stage and apotheosis of the 18th century symphony as we know it in the imperishable last works in that form that were bequeathed to us by Haydn and Mozart.

---

[1] Leopold Mozart said that "half-composers" often did this, meaning composers who were not technically well equipped.

II

THE FRENCH OUVERTURE AND THE ITALIAN SINFONIA

PERFORMANCES of masque, opera, ballet, oratorio, cantata, or indeed of almost any form of dramatic work in which music was employed, have from their very beginnings generally been ushered in by some sort of instrumental introduction. By the end of the 17th century these introductions had assumed two distinct forms, and were known, respectively, as the French *Ouverture* and the Italian *Sinfonia*. Although they differed in plan and style, both served the same purpose, and both provided the ingredients for the future concert-symphony. The concert-symphony was created when an *Ouverture* or a *Sinfonia* was detached from the main body of the work to which it served as an instrumental introduction, and was played separately, for its own sake, as a piece of concert-music. The overture and the symphony, as we now understand these words, must therefore share the same early history.

Similar works in one or other of these two forms, and indistinguishable from their prototypes, but existing independently of any opera, oratorio or other work, were being written during the first half of the 18th century, and the output, which began as a trickle, increased greatly after the mid-century, and during the 'fifties, 'sixties and 'seventies had become so profuse as to defy any attempt at enumeration. It was not until towards the close of the century that the overture and the symphony again became clearly distinguishable and that those two words assumed their present meanings; the overture was then understood to be an instrumental introduction to some larger work, and the symphony stood by itself as a work intended for concert-performance and unattached to any opera, oratorio or other vocal or dramatic work.

The French *Ouverture* took shape and became an established form during the second half of the 17th century; it is well typified in the overtures to the operas and ballets written for the French court by Lulli during the period 1662 to 1686. The general plan was Slow-Quick-Slow (*Lentement-Vitement-Lentement*), and the strongest characteristics were (*a*) a short, slow and stately introductory movement, largely based on the rhythm ♩. ♪ , followed by (*b*) a longer and lively fugal Allegro, which was generally concluded by a return for a few bars to the original slow tempo. If anything more was added, it was commonly a Minuet, Gavotte, Gigue or other dance form, or possibly a march; but the hall-mark and indispensable distinguishing features of the *Ouverture* were the slow introduction and the ensuing fugal Allegro.

This form preserved its identity throughout the first half of the 18th century, but was then no longer associated with only French opera and ballet. German, Italian and English composers also made free use of it, not only to introduce their stage-works, but also to precede their oratorios. Of some 66 opera and oratorio overtures by Handel, all except eight are in the form of the French *Ouverture*,[1] sometimes modified, but always easily recognisable as an enlarged form of the Lullian overture; some of them came to an end after the fugal Allegro (*Messiah*), but most of them include a third movement in the form of a Minuet, Gavotte, Gigue, Bourrée, March, or sometimes a short lively Allegro in compound time.

The same form of overture was often adopted by both German and Italian composers to introduce their operas written for the German theatres, as for example, by Keiser at Hamburg, Hasse at Dresden, the two Grauns at Berlin and Schürmann at Brunswick. It also became the model for many instrumental works that were self-contained and entirely independent of any opera or oratorio; the North German composer, Telemann, is said to have written about 600 of these unattached overtures, and others, including J. S. Bach, Johann Friedrich Fasch, Christoph Förster and Johann Schneider used the same form for the initial movements of their instrumental Suites.

Lulli's overtures were short and slight;[2] the rather watery counterpoint in the fugal Allegros is formal and stiff, and the movements seem to come to an end almost before they have

---

[1] Exceptions are: *Acis and Galatea*, 2nd overture to *Solomon, Parnasso*, 1st and 2nd overtures to *Saul, Lotharius, Deborah* and the *Coronation Anthem*.

[2] Lulli, overture to *Atys*, ed. and arr. by Adam Carse (Music for School Orchestra), Augener Ltd.

really got into their stride. The same might be said of Lulli's contemporaries and immediate successors, but Purcell's overtures were made of stronger stuff, and are probably the best of all 17th century overtures. Rameau strengthened the French *Ouverture*, and a good English example is the overture to Arne's *Masque of Comus* (1738).

In the hands of the German composers the *Ouverture* gained both length and substance; the heavier tread of the German style, although often inclined to become academic and stodgy, brought to the music a certain solidity and dignity which was well suited to the character and texture of the fugal Allegro, even if it was at the cost of the airy grace which characterized the native French style. But when the *Ouverture* was treated with the robust vigour and innate skill of a Handel and a Bach, the old form acquired warmth and life such as it had never enjoyed in the country of its origin.

After the mid-century the French *Ouverture* began to go out of favour, but although steadily losing ground, it never became quite extinct. Writing in 1752, Quantz said that the *Ouverture* was already no longer customary (*üblich*) in Germany. But it is easily recognizable, for example, in Mozart's overture to *Die Zauberflöte*, with its slow introduction and fugal Allegro, now shaped to conform to the general plan of the prevailing Sonata Form. Even in the 19th century the old *Ouverture* still survived, and was sometimes called upon to supply the instrumental introduction to oratorios, as in Mendelssohn's *Elijah* and *St. Paul*.

The Italian *Sinfonia* took shape a little later than the French *Ouverture*, but had become an established form by the beginning of the 18th century. Alessandro Scarlatti, in his later operas, provides examples of the *Sinfonia* in its early and typical form, although the plan may perhaps be traced back to some of his predecessors, such as Perti and Stradella. The general design was Quick-Slow-Quick, or Allegro-Andante-Presto. During the greater part of the 18th century this short three-movement form was used for countless Italian operas, whether written by Italians, Germans, or composers of any other nationality, and these, when detached from the operas to which they belonged, were often used as concert-symphonies, just in the same way as were the French overtures. Many old printed and MS bound collections of the part-books of such works point very clearly to the constant use of these detached pieces for concert purposes.

Scarlatti's *Sinfonias* had in their make-up much of the elements of the Concerto, in which a distinction is made between solo and ripieno parts, but the typical opera *Sinfonia* had by the middle of the 18th century become more truly orchestral in style, and with some increase in length, had by then settled down to a more or less standardized design which may be summarized as follows: an Allegro, usually in Common Time, of about 80 to 120 bars, energetic, showy and fully scored; an Andante which might contain from 30 to 80 bars (varying according to the length of the bar), lyrical and quietly scored; a final Presto of 100 or more bars, usually in 3/8 time, bustling and fully scored. The whole might occupy only six or seven minutes in performance, and generally gives the impression that it had been manufactured according to a standard pattern without the exercise of any invention or originality, and with all the signs of haste and impatience to get the job done as quickly as possible. The composers seem to have put down the first thing that came into their heads, and were no doubt well aware that nobody listened to the overture and would only show some interest in the music—or the performers—when the singing began.

An increase in the length of the opera *Sinfonia* after the mid-century was mainly due to the fact that Sonata Form was then taking possession of the first movement, and (when it was not a Rondo) of the Finale as well.

These little three-movement opera *Sinfonias* are indistinguishable from the concert-symphonies that were being written about the same time, and many of them figured in both capacities, as for example, in one of the collections of six published symphonies by Johann Christian Bach and in Arne's overtures. The words symphony and overture had by then become virtually synonymous, and in this country the publishers, following the practice of those at Amsterdam and Paris, issued what they called " periodical overtures " in monthly numbers, naming them overtures on the outside cover and symphonies on the first page of the music.

If the three-movement Italian opera *Sinfonia* is not often heard nowadays, it is not for any lack of examples, but rather because not many of them are to be had in modern print and adapted for performance under present conditions. Vast numbers of the overtures may be found in libraries all over Europe, sometimes attached to, and sometimes detached from their operas, in MS and in print, mostly written by composers whose music has long since gone out of use. Some of the composers' names are familiar enough to readers of musical histories, some can still be found in Musical Dictionaries, while others have left no trace of their existence except a few mute scores which lie undisturbed amongst the relics of a past that is more remarkable for the quantity than the quality of its music. The names of Jommelli, Piccini, Sacchini, Pugnani, to mention only a typical few, are well remembered even if their music is rarely heard; such as Guglielmi, Sarti, Celestino, Anfossi and a few dozen others can be looked up in Grove or Riemann; but who were Riso, Cavi, Danesi, or a score of others whose names are to be found only in a few library catalogues? Non-Italian composers also contributed largely to the output of three-movement opera *Sinfonias*. Such as J. Chris. Bach and Anton Filtz amongst the Germans and Bohemians, Gossec amongst the French or Belgians, and Arne, Storace and Linley amongst the Englishmen, together with others whose names alone would fill a page or two of this book, all helped to swell the vast store of forgotten overtures in the form of the Italian *Sinfonia*, which will be found only by those who are willing to hunt for them in libraries where old music is preserved. A good and typical English *Sinfonia* is the overture to *The Duenna* by Thomas Linley jun.[1]

Although there is generally a clear distinction between the French *Ouverture* and the Italian *Sinfonia*, it should not be expected that every single overture written in the 18th century will fall easily into one or other of these two classes. There are instances of the fusion of the two types in such a way that, having some of the characteristics of each, it becomes impossible to classify them. The *Sinfonia*, for example, might borrow the slow introduction from the *Ouverture*,[2] or it might substitute a Minuet for the more usual final Presto. Handel's

---
[1] 18th C.O.
[2] See Scarlatti, overture to *La Rosaura* (Music for School Orchestras) Augener Ltd.

first overture to *Saul*, for example, is obviously a hybrid, containing an *Ouverture* within a *Sinfonia:* Allegro (non-fugal) —Larghetto—Fugal Allegro—Andante—March.

The real fusion of the two types only begins when the concert-symphony, written as such, comes into being during the first half of the 18th century. The material was all ready to hand; the Italian *Sinfonia* was taken over wholesale, thus providing the first Allegro, the slow movement and the quick Finale, while the French *Ouverture* contributed the slow introduction and the Minuet. The fugal Allegro of the *Ouverture* was rejected; the slow introduction was not always included, and when it was, it became part of the first movement, while the Minuet crept in gradually, and eventually became an integral part of the four-movement concert-symphony as we know it in the well-known works of Haydn and Mozart.

Towards the end of the 18th century the three-movement opera Sinfonia was being gradually discarded in favour of the one-movement overture in Sonata Form, a type particularly associated with Italian *opera buffa*, and at that point the histories of the overture and the symphony finally part company.

The form of each movement will be treated in a later chapter, but before that is attempted, the appearance and growth of the independent concert-symphony must be considered.

III

THE INDEPENDENT CONCERT-SYMPHONY

WHEN composers found that the *Ouverture* or *Sinfonia* was often being diverted from its original purpose as an instrumental prelude to some opera or other work, and was being made use of as a concert-piece, it is not surprising that they should have begun to write pieces designed on similar lines and intended for performance as instrumental items on occasions when no stage-work or oratorio was being produced.

The reader who knows anything about musical life and conditions in the earlier part of the 18th century may quite justifiably put the question: as there were no public orchestral concerts in those days, where and when, or on what sort of occasions were these pieces performed? It is true that there were no public orchestral concerts at which a symphony and a concerto, flanked by a couple of overtures, were the central items in the programme, and to which anybody might gain admission by payment; but there were plenty of other occasions for which a symphony or an overture was considered indispensable, indeed, most musical functions began and ended with some such instrumental work.

The musicians employed at the many courts, large and small, of which there were hundreds almost all over Europe, and especially in the German-speaking states, in Bohemia and Hungary, even if less numerous in France and other countries, were constantly playing in the private chambers of the sovereigns or petty rulers who employed them, and all of those required a considerable repertoire of instrumental pieces. Then, every theatre, even though not producing opera, had its orchestra to play before the rise of the curtain and between the acts, and there was little else for them to play but these short overtures or symphonies. Concert-societies, usually run on a subscription basis, if few in the first half of the century, increased in number after the mid-century; such as the

Concert Spirituel, the *Concert des Amateurs,* the *Concert de la Loge Olympique* in Paris, the beginnings of the *Gewandhaus* concerts at Leipzig, the Bach-Abel Concerts, the *Professional Concert* and the Haydn-Salomon concerts in London, are only some of the most prominent institutions at which symphonies and overtures were regularly played, at least two in every programme.

All of these, however, would not have sufficed to absorb the immense output of symphonies that was being written and published in the second half of the century. The existence of numerous sets of orchestral parts, in MS and printed, and often in bound part-books, clearly implies that there must have been very many more small orchestras than are recorded in musical history, and that these little bodies, playing in comparative obscurity, had an insatiable appetite for the copious supply of overtures and symphonies that composers and publishers were ready to provide for them. The Leipzig publisher, Breitkopf, found that it was worth while issuing a thematic catalogue, reissued and amplified from time to time (1762-1787), of the works for which they were prepared to supply copies in the form of MS parts; and this was done not only for a dozen or two prominent concert-giving institutions; the field was obviously much larger, and must have covered numerous small performing bodies of which we have no records.

But the most convincing proof of the existence of so many performing orchestras lies in the fact that the music publishers were willing and able to engrave and issue symphonies and overtures in seemingly endless profusion. The flow in the first half of the century was somewhat limited, but from about 1760 to 1800 there must have been a heavy demand for these works " in eight parts," and they were forthcoming in amazing quantities from the publishers in Amsterdam, Berlin, Leipzig, Paris, London, and rather later in Vienna, in a form which could have been used only for actual performance, and not for any other purpose. When Walsh in London printed separately the orchestral parts of over 60 overtures by Handel, it was because there was a use for them in that form; and when the later publishers kept up a constant supply of such printed parts, and kept on re-issuing them, it was not that they were actuated by artistic zeal or were doing it to please the composers; it was because they could sell the parts and keep on selling them. Had there been little use for them, the supply would soon have dried up; but far from drying up, it went forward and increased in volume until the time came when the later symphonies of Haydn and Mozart, and finally the appearance of Beethoven's symphonies, put the work of the earlier symphonists so completely in the shade that their works faded out of use and the music remained to become little more than useless lumber that was either destroyed or eventually found its way into libraries, museums or private collections.

If it is asked: when did composers begin to write the independent concert-symphonies? no answer can be given. Even an exhaustive examination of hundreds of works in dozens of libraries would not provide enlightenment, for unless a work can be dated with certainty, the chronology must always be vague and speculative. Nothing is more difficult than to date a piece of old music, and if the composer is not one of the "great," the means of arriving at any satisfactory conclusion have by now probably dissappeared and the task has been rendered practically impossible. Not much more can be said than that composers were writing independent symphonies or overtures well before the middle of the 18th century, it may have been even before the beginning of that century.

Of those that were certainly written before 1750, one might instance the " Eight Overtures in eight parts for Violins, Hoboys, French Horns etc., with a through Bass for the Harpsicord or Violoncello " (Walsh 1740 ?), by Giuseppe St. Martini, better known as Sammartini. The first four of these are French *Ouvertures* with a march or some other lively movement as a conclusion. No. 1 has a slow introduction of 20 bars, beginning in D and ending in A major; the fugal Allegro in D has 123 bars, and a march-like Finale in D is a binary movement of 76 bars. The last four of Martini's " Overtures or Concertos " are in the form of the Italian *Sinfonia*. No. 5 opens with a binary non-fugal Allegro of 64 bars in D; and Andante in B minor occupies only eight bars in 12/8 time, the final Allegro comprises 330 bars in

3/8 time, and a short "Marcia" of 44 bars is thrown in, no doubt as a makeweight for the unusually short Andante. No. 6 begins with an Allegro assai in G major in 3/8 time (215 bars); then comes an Andante of 18 bars in G minor, then a Minuetto in 3/8, a Trio in G minor, and a return to the Minuetto, the whole occupying about 154 bars without counting the repeats and the *Da Capo*.

Of Pasquali's "XII Overtures and Symphonies" (*c*. 1740–1750), eight are in the Italian and four in the French form; six of them were actual overtures to dramatic works, but the remaining six were presumably written as independent concert-pieces. Another set belonging to the same period is Arne's "Eight Overtures in 8 parts," published by Walsh about 1740. These are mainly on the model of the French *Ouverture*, but Nos. 3 and 5 follow the plan of the *Sinfonia;* No. 7 is actually the overture to *Comus* (French *Ouverture*), and No. 8 is the overture to *The Judgement of Paris*,[1] also a French *Ouverture* with a Minuet and a Gigue. No. 4 of this set,[2] which again is an *Ouverture*, has an unusually long slow introduction (42 bars), followed by a fugal Allegro (with episodes) of 65 bars, and concludes with what is really a Minuet without a trio occupying 40 bars. The whole work takes about seven minutes to perform.[3] Another and later set of Arne's is the "Four new Overtures or Symphonies, in 8 and 10 parts, for Violins, Tenors, Oboes, Horns, Flutes etc., calculated for Public or Private Concerts." These are modelled on the Italian *Sinfonia*, and it may be noted that Arne treats the words overture and symphony as meaning one and the same thing.

Up to that time (*c*. 1740) composers of symphonies had to follow the plan of either the *Ouverture* or the *Sinfonia*, unless, as sometimes occurred, they chose to mix the features of the two types in some hybrid form.

The further development of the symphony was then due to be carried on under the influence of the gradually emerging so-called Sonata Form. Like all other musical growths, this was evolved gradually and according to no ordered plan, and therefore cannot be precisely dated, but it might be put in this way: it would be difficult or impossible to find a movement in Sonata Form that was written much before 1740, and it

---

[1] 18th C.O.   [2] B.C.S.   [3] For full analysis, see p. 51.

would be very unusual to find a first movement of a symphony composed after 1775 that was not in Sonata Form.

Concomitant with the gradual change in form came an equally gradual change in the style and texture of instrumental music, a metamorphosis that may be represented, for example, by the change from Bach's way of writing for instruments to that of Mozart. The contrapuntal conception of music was innate in all composers whose maturity coincided with the earlier part of the 18th century, and this was gradually transformed from a contrapuntal way of thinking into a texture wherein melody and its harmonic accompaniment constitute the normal state or condition of the music, while nevertheless retaining some of the elements of contrapuntal movement, such as, for example, imitation, or the transference of the melodic part into the bass or some other than the uppermost part. The new music was, as it is often expressed, in the *galante* style, and was transparent, easily grasped, light-hearted, and free from the grind of continuous contrapuntal part-writing.

In so far as it relates to symphonies, early signs of the change appeared in the works of Johann Stamitz (1717-1757), the leader and inspirer of the Mannheim group of symphonists whose works then became the model for most other composers of symphonies, whose orchestral style influenced Mozart, and which subsisted until the whole thing was taken completely out of their hands by the infinite superiority of the example of Haydn and Mozart.

Stamitz was at Mannheim from 1741 until his death, but in 1754-5 he spent some time in Paris in close touch with La Pouplinière, a rich tax-farmer who kept a private orchestra, and there introduced the German-style symphony into France.

Johann Stamitz's symphony in G, Op. 3, No. 3,[1] is planned on the model of the Italian *Sinfonia* in three movements: Allegro—Andantino—Presto. The tentative Sonata Form shows itself here in a work which looks both backwards and forwards, a symphony, so to speak, at the crossroads, lingering with the old yet venturing into the new, but treading carefully and making no bold experiments.[2] In the first movement of No. 2 in D of the same opus number[3] there is a clearly defined Second Subject in the dominant key in the exposition, and

[1] E.C.S.   [2] For analysis of the form, see p. 51.   [3] In score in the D.D.T.

this reappears transposed into the tonic key towards the end of the movement without having made any formal recapitulation of the first or principal subject. This is a four-movement work with a Minuet and Trio: Presto, 4/4, 125 bars—Andantino, 2/4, 62 bars—Minuet and Trio, 36 bars—Prestissimo, 3/8, 187 bars.

Amongst the elder Stamitz's pupils or disciples, and directly influenced by his work, were Chris. Cannabich, Ignaz Fränzl, Anton Filtz, Carl Stamitz, Franz Beck and the two Toëschis, all of them string players and at some time members of the Mannheim orchestra. Their symphonies, which belong to the third quarter of the century, are much in the same tradition as those of Stamitz, but rather lighter in style and texture, terse and compact, feeling their way towards full Sonata Form, but still clinging to much that was characteristic of the old Italian *Sinfonia*. Filtz's symphony in E flat and Carlo Giuseppe Toëschi's symphony in D[1] are typical specimens of the short three-movement concert-symphonies occupying ten to twelve minutes in performance which were then being turned out in large numbers not only by the Mannheim adherents, but also by many other composers who apparently took the Mannheim symphonies as their model even though their musical outlook was not inherited direct from the Elector Karl Theodore's famous musical establishment.

Ignaz Holzbauer (1711–1783), composer of 65 symphonies, although he became a Mannheim *Kapellmeister*, can hardly be counted a disciple of Stamitz, but takes his place with Wagenseil, Reutter and Monn amongst the earlier of the Viennese symphonists. His symphony in E flat[2] became well-known, probably because of the last movement which represents a storm at sea (*La Tempesta del Mare*), and is a four-movement work with a Minuet and Trio, revealing more German solidity and a closer-wrought texture than the works of Filtz and Toëschi, albeit without their easy grace. F. Xaver Richter and Georg Tzarth (Czarth), although both associated with Mannheim, were not so much disciples as contemporaries of the elder Stamitz.

The Belgian-born Gossec, however, may be counted among those who were directly influenced by Stamitz, and was probably the first " French " composer to write German

---
[1]Both in E.C.S.   [2]E.C.S.

symphonies. Gossec was employed in La Pouplinière's orchestra in 1751, the very year in which one of Stamitz's symphonies was first performed in Paris at the *Concert Spirituel*. His symphonies, numbering over thirty, date from 1759 to 1778, thus beginning soon after Stamitz had come to Paris and was there closely associated with La Pouplinière's orchestra; the connection was therefore direct and probably very close. Gossec's symphony in D,[1] Allegro—Andante un poco Allegretto—Presto, obviously owes much to Stamitz in respect of form and lay-out, but the temper of the music is more highly-strung than that of the steady-going conscientious German-Bohemian.

Another symphonist of Belgian birth, Pierre van Maldere (1729–1768)[2] may possibly be considered an indirect disciple of Stamitz, for he was (according to Gassner) in Paris in 1754 just when Stamitz was there teaching the Parisians to understand and appreciate the German symphony. At least 24 of his symphonies were published in Brussels, Paris and London, and are said to have been very popular before Haydn's works in that form had become known. Maldere's symphony in B flat, Op. IV, No. 3,[3] has some vitality and contains a well-made Andante that makes an appeal by means of its genuinely expressive feeling.

The first movements of the symphonies hitherto noticed show how Sonata Form was clearly taking shape, yet was still growing. In these, when the tonic key is resumed after any development that there may be, it is not to recapitulate the First Subject just as it appeared at the beginning of the movement; the matter used in the transition is picked up at some point between the beginning of the movement and the Second Subject, and then leads to a re-statement of the Second Subject, now diverted into the tonic key. These symphonies are contemporary with the early symphonies of Haydn and Mozart, in which the form of the first movement is very similarly planned.

During the 'sixties and 'seventies the output of symphonies was so copious as to render it hardly possible to even name all of the composers, much less to notice all their works. It would not be difficult to name fifty composers who wrote symphonies, generally in batches of six at a time, many of

---
[2] Some of the earlier Musical Dictionaries appear to have confused Pierre van Maldere with his brother.
[1] E.C.S.   [3] E.C.S.

18th CENTURY SYMPHONIES   21

whom could claim to have composed from 30 to 50 or more such works. Even if it were possible to comment on all these works, the record would be tedious and useless, and would involve much repetition and uninteresting detail. Only a few of them need be particularised, and the choice will be of those composers by whom at least one work is now easily accessible in full score.

Among those whose symphonies were very popular in their day one might pick out Johann Christian Bach (1735–1782) and Carl Friedrich Abel (1725–1787), two musicians who were closely associated with concert-giving in London from 1764 to 1782 while both were resident in this country. The list of his works in Terry's *John Christian Bach* shows that there are over thirty of his symphonies or overtures in print and twenty-four in MS. Many of them served both as concert-symphonies and opera-overtures, and it is impossible to say whether the composer helped himself to a symphony when in want of an opera-overture or *vice versa*. The printed symphonies are all short three-movement works on the plan of the Italian *Sinfonia*, occupying some six or seven minutes in performance, with a Minuet occasionally substituted for the final Presto. Bach's symphony in B flat,[1] the third of a set of three (Op. 21 ?), published at The Hague, Paris, and twice in London, is a gay and elegant little work imbued with a sunny spirit which seems to reflect the composers Italian apprenticeship as well as his indolent character and light-hearted artistic outlook. In this work the Second Subject is in the dominant key both in the Exposition and the Recapitulation, and there is really no Development. The Finale is a Rondo on a very small scale, and is over in about a minute and a half. Three of J. C. Bach's symphonies,[2] and another which also figures as the overture to *Orione*,[3] are available in score in modern editions, and yet another is amongst those issued and "*bearbeitet*" by Dr. Sondheimer.[4] Mozart's first symphonies are generally said to have been modelled on those of J. C. Bach, with whom he was in contact in 1764 when Leopold Mozart brought Wolfgang and his sister to London in order to exploit their precocity.

In Abel's symphony in E flat, Op. 10, No. 3,[5] the main theme of which presages that of Beethoven's *Eroica*, the

---
[1]E.C.S.   [2]Peter's ed.
[3]Oxford Univ. Press; essential bassoon parts are missing in this score.
[4]Edition Bernoulli, Berlin.   [5]E.C.S.

First Subject reappears after a development of 48 bars exactly as it was at the beginning of the movement; the Recapitulation, in fact, is the Exposition all over again except for the change of key and the two concluding bars: Exposition, 62 bars—Development, 48 bars—Recapitulation, 64 bars. Abel's symphonies are contemporary with those of J. C. Bach; if they lack the elegance of the latter, they have more substance and are thoroughly German in spirit. Yet the two composers had much in common and designed their symphonies much on the same scale, making their greatest effort in the first movement, relaxing into gentle lyricism in the second, and scampering through the Finale quickly and with little thought, as if they were anxious to get the job done as soon as possible.

In the meantime, while these little symphonies were being poured out in half-dozens at a time, a young man named Joseph Haydn had taken up his first appointment as *Kapellmeister* to Count Morzin in 1759, and in that year composed his first symphony, just about two years after the death of Johann Stamitz. Haydn was no innovator; he took the symphony as he found it, and, no doubt keeping an eye on what other composers were doing, let it grow and develop without apparent effort but with the urge of a strong and fluent creative gift and an instinctive musicianship which, when combined, soon placed his symphonies on a higher plane than those of his contemporaries, and at the same time managed to please the ears and the taste of those who heard them. Apparently using the same sort of material in much the same way as other composers, he made—if such a homely phrase may be permitted—a better job of it. Already in 1764 the parts of some of his earlier symphonies were being engraved and published by Chevardière and Venier in Paris,[1] and his reputation was beginning to spread further afield than Eisenstadt and Esterhaz, where he was now working for his patron-prince. The early symphonies are planned on the lines of the three-movement Italian *Sinfonia*, but sometimes a Minuet is added and occasionally a slow introduction ushers in the first Allegro. Yet, although they were better than most, the first fifty or so of Haydn's symphonies (1759-1772) did not reach a level that was high enough to cause his rivals

---

[1] G. A. Nos. 1, 2, 5, 12, 14.

in the same field to retreat in dismay. So the manufacture of symphonies went on as merrily and as copiously as ever before.

When in 1764 Haydn's symphonies were approaching his thirtieth, an eight-year-old boy named Wolfgang Amadeus Mozart was in London composing his first symphony and also copying out a few others, one or two of which were for a long time mistaken for his own. The eight-year-old, of course, could do no more than take the symphony as he found it, and his models appear to have been the works of J. C. Bach and Abel, both of whom were then resident in London. When the young Mozart had, so to speak, got his hand in, he brought to bear on his symphonic writing a gift so strong and one which developed so quickly that he soon drew level with Haydn. By the time Haydn had reached his fiftieth (1772), Mozart had written his twenty-second symphony,[1] and if the last few of these had become more widely known and played, it is possible that what may be called " the rout of the 18th century symphonists " might have occurred some years earlier than it did. But while Haydn's symphonies were being disseminated and were already widely appreciated, Mozart's remained in comparative obscurity in the hands of those for whom he wrote them.

The pair of them, Haydn and Mozart, were destined to write symphonies that eventually obliterated the entire output of the mob of 18th century symphonists, but that time had not yet come, and a crowd of composers continued to spawn symphonies in blissful ignorance of the fate that awaited their offspring. Most of their names will be found in the list at the end of this book, and in the meantime a few more works that are easily accessible in score will be noticed.

Friedrich Schwindl (*d.* 1786) was a South German whose instrumental works seem to have enjoyed widespread popularity in the 'seventies and 'eighties, especially in London, where several of his symphonies were published by Bremner and Wornum. The symphony in F[2] is a bright and genial little work, and reveals the composer's ability to develop his material. Here, again, the Exposition and Recapitulation are identical in length and design (56 bars), and there is a

---

[1] The numbering in both cases is that of the G.A.   [2] E.C.S.

dainty second Subject in five-bar groups, and a minute but graceful Coda.

A prolific writer of symphonies, a better musician than most, and more ambitious, was Carl von Dittersdorf (1739-1799). His symphony *dans le genre de cinq Nations* was published in Paris in 1767, and three of his twelve symphonies on Ovid's *Metamorphoses*, an early instance of symphonies with a poetical background, were issued by Artaria at Vienna in 1785, and reprinted by Reinecke at Leipzig in 1899. The "favourite" symphony in C,[1] "as performed at Mr. Kammell's Subscription Concerts with universal applause," is probably a fairly early work, but reveals some skill and musicianship in the handling of the themes in the Development, which, with some show of imagination, places the composer a degree or two above the rank and file of his contemporaries; indeed, had it not been for Haydn and Mozart, Dittersdorf might have ranked with Boccherini amongst the best of the 18th century symphonists.

During the late 'seventies and early 'eighties the symphony was expanding both in length and substance. The Minuet, first introduced by the early Viennese and Mannheim composers, was now generally included, and a slow introduction sometimes preceded the first Allegro. The Development was getting longer, and the Coda, although still short, was growing. But, above all, the last movement was expanding far beyond the dimensions of such as J. C. Bach's and Abel's miniature Finales. The old Italian *Sinfonia* was now being left behind, and the ten-minute symphony-overture was becoming a twenty-minute concert-symphony. The mass-production of these works was still in progress, and some years had yet to pass before it was halted towards the end of the century.

Mozart's contribution during this period—roughly 1774 to 1784—includes several works that were destined to outlive all the symphonies of the "mob," as well as most of Haydn's written during the same period. The young composer was outrunning the older one, and his output included such significant works as No. 29 in A, the "Paris" (a landmark in the history of the symphony), No. 34 in C, the "Haffner" and the "Linz" symphonies. But these works, although

---
[1] E.C.S.

standing head and shoulders above the contemporary output, could hardly exert any influence on the development of the symphony as long as their circulation was restricted. Only three of Mozart's symphonies were published (in parts) during his lifetime, and there is all the difference in the world between the influence that may be exerted by a MS. work reposing in somebody's library and a printed work circulating in many countries.

Haydn's output during the same period (Nos. 51 to 81) includes a few symphonies that are still occasionally played, also some that are not yet available in modern print; but the circulation of these works was much more widespread than in the case of Mozart; indeed, most of them were already in print by 1784, and some had appeared three or four times in Vienna, Amsterdam, Paris and London. Haydn's reputation was by then very considerable, and was just about to bring him an invitation to write symphonies for the *Concert de la Loge Olympique* at Paris, and later on, for London.

The Paris symphonies added still more to Haydn's reputation, and it was not long before all of them were available in print. The time of their composition is that which just precedes the year in which Mozart wrote his last three great symphonies. The group includes such as No. 82 (*L'Ours*), No. 83 (*La Poule*), No. 85 (*La Reine*) and No. 86, and they were scored for a larger orchestra, including flute, oboes, bassoons, horns, and in some cases trumpets and drums as well. The last movements were now longer, and gave the whole a better proportioned balance in relation to the other movements.

The final stage of the story of the 18th century symphony may be epitomised in the following: Mozart—the " Prague," 1786; the E flat major, G minor and " Jupiter " (1788); Haydn—the " Oxford," 1788; the twelve London symphonies, 1791–1795.

Again, the younger man was ahead of the older in point of date, but in the former case the publishing and circulating proceeded more leisurely and delayed the full appreciation of Mozart's last and greatest symphonies until Haydn's last twelve were already launched in London and were soon after being issued in printed form from the presses of Artaria (Vienna), André (Offenbach) and Forster (London).

The last word had been said in the history of the 18th century symphony, and as these works began to circulate the rout of the remaining symphonists began. Dittersdorf, Pugnani, Kozeluch, Boccherini, Pleyel and a few others were still in the field during the last few years of the century, and their works lingered for some years even in the early 19th century; but, together with the mob of the 'sixties and 'seventies, they too were overwhelmed by the avalanche of Haydn's and Mozart's last symphonies, and when Beethoven began to turn out the first few of his immortal nine, the rout was complete and no more was heard of the crowd of composers who had taken a share in the making of the symphony, but whose work was now being discarded just as the scaffolding is dismantled when a building is completed.

The symphony would never have reached the stage in its development to which Haydn and Mozart brought it in their last works had it remained solely in their hands, indeed, neither would ever have composed a symphony had it not been already an established form at the time when they began their work, respectively, in 1759 and 1764. Stamitz, J. C. Bach, Abel, and many others had already more than laid the foundation before the two great Viennese masters began to build on it; they had erected enough of the superstructure to make quite clear the lines on which it was to develop, and on which Haydn and Mozart were able to build and lead to its culmination during the last two decades of the century. Mozart would never have created the symphony out of nothing had he not found it ready-made in London in 1764, flourishing at Mannheim in 1777, and appreciated at Paris in 1778; and Haydn would not have gone on writing symphonies from 1759 to 1795 without the vast background of activity that was feeding and stimulating the demand for a continuous supply of these works during the whole of his active life.

It takes many composers to make one good one, and it required hundreds of symphonies from which the essence had to be distilled before the accumulation of experience and effort blossomed and flowered late in the 18th century. The spadework was done by a host of composers whose works have long been forgotten, and without it the symphony as we now know it would never have existed.

A few words about the programme-symphony may be added to this brief history. Symphonies with a literary or dramatic background, some of which present naïve attempts at realism, and some which exploit merely imitative sounds, were by no means uncommon in the 18th century. Holzbauer's " Storm at Sea," Dittersdorf's " Five Nations " and " Metamorphoses " symphonies have already been mentioned; Koch (*Lexikon*) also mentions symphonies on the " Four Ages " and " The Fall of Phaeton " by the same composer, one entitled " Telemach " by Rosetti, and he includes in this category Haydn's " The Seven Last Words." Mennicke[1] alludes to programme-symphonies by Raimondi, Mysliweczek, Rosetti and Pichl. To these may be added Hunting symphonies by Haydn, Gossec, Carl Stamitz, Wilh. Cramer and Méhul, in which hunting calls on the French horns are " featured." The nicknames attached to so many of Haydn's symphonies do not imply any particular programme or conscious attempts to make the music tell a story, depict a scene or describe an event; they generally associate the work with a prevailing feeling, a person, place, or supposed likeness in it to some natural or other sound, and were no doubt mainly useful in identifying particular works when there was no regularised way of numbering them.

---

[1] *Hasse und die Brüder Graun als Symphoniker* (1906).

IV

THE FORM OF THE MOVEMENTS

THE introductory slow movement of the French *Ouverture* was held together by its rhythm rather than by thematic cohesion. It was in quadruple time, and might occupy from ten to twenty bars in which the dominating rhythmical pattern was a long note followed by a short note or a group of short notes. In actual notation the long note might appear as either a dotted note, a tied note, or a note followed by a rest, and the short note would be a quaver or its value in shorter notes. Contemporary theorists made it clear that the dotted note should be sustained beyond its actual value (the double dot was not then in use), and that the short note or notes should be played as quickly as possible.

It was this rhythmical unity that served to keep together music which is little more than a harmonic progress through one or two related keys, ending with either a full close in the dominant key or a half close in the tonic key; the whole was usually repeated and furnished with First and Second Time bars.

The 18th century theorists always emphasised the festive and spirited character of the introductory movement. Although the *tempo* was slow, the effect was to be " magnificent and solemn " (Quantz), " earnest but fiery " (Sulzer), " noble but lively," " sublime," " elevated," and so on. The movement was often marked *Spiritoso*.

The ensuing fugal Allegro might be in duple, triple or quadruple time, and might be a regular (strict) fugue, an irregular (free) fugue, or merely imitative part-writing. Most of these movements are fugal only in the sense that they start off with the successive entry of the parts, as in a fugal exposition, and that the main idea makes periodical entries throughout the movement; but they are not usually strict fugues in that the parts may also be employed in merely supplying the harmony, and that episodes of a non-fugal character

18th CENTURY SYMPHONIES

may occur. There is, of course, no fixed plan or order of entry, and no particular form apart from the inevitable progress away from the tonic and dominant keys through a few related keys, and a final return to the tonic key. The movement generally ends with a few bars of harmonic progression in slow *tempo*, making a full close in the tonic key.

Contemporary theorists all remark on the lively character of the fugal Allegro; it should be "fresh and lively" (Mattheson), "a brilliant and well-wrought movement" (Quantz); Rousseau used the words "skipping" and "gay" to describe its character. The fugal Allegro of the earlier or Lullian *Ouverture* occupied only about 30 or 40 bars, but in the hands of the Germans, who began to use it before the end of the 17th century, it acquired a more imposing length and a better-wrought texture. In Handel's overtures the fugal Allegro generally ran to 60 or 70 bars, and in Bach's Suites from about 80 to well over 100 bars. When a Minuet, Gigue or other movement was appended, it usually took the form that was basic in most instrumental movements dating from the earlier part of the 18th century, namely, the two-part or Binary form that was built up on one central theme; otherwise it might be a three-part form, also based on one dominating idea.

Good examples of the earlier French *Ouverture* may be found in Lulli's overtures to *Atys*[1] and *Thessée*,[2] and in Purcell's overture to *Dioclesian*.[3] Of the larger 18th century type, the most familiar examples are the overtures that begin Bach's orchestral Suites, and most of Handel's overtures.

Sometimes the first part of an *Ouverture* was expanded into a movement which was more than an introductory preamble, as in the case of Handel's overture to *Esther* (26 bars),[4] and Arne's symphony-overture No. 4 in F (42 bars).[5] These two and Arne's overture to *The Judgement of Paris*[6] provide excellent examples of the extended fugal Allegro with episodes.

The two-part form already referred to is proportioned and balanced mainly by its tonality (key-relationship) and the treatment of one central idea which may consist of little more than a melodic figure possessing an easily recognisable shape and possibly some rhythmical or metrical characteristic of

---
[1] *Music for School Orchestra*, ed. and arr. by Adam Carse (Augener Ltd.).
[2] *The Amateur Orchestra* (Joseph Williams Ltd.).
[3] *Ibid.*   [4] 18th C.O.   [5] F.C.S.   [6] 18th C.O.

its own. The movement is divided into two parts, of which the second is usually the longer, by a cadence at the end of the first part which causes a temporary halt in the progress of the music, and is commonly either a full close in the dominant key or a half close in the tonic key; the division is often marked by a double bar and repeat sign. When the movement is in a minor key the modulation may be to the relative major instead of to the dominant key.[1] The second part usually starts with the central theme transposed into the dominant key, and then proceeds through one or more related keys which sooner or later lead back to the tonic key. There is no recapitulation of the music with which the movement began, and the conclusion is generally a transposition into the tonic key of the cadence or the last few bars that marked the end of the first part. (See Example I, page 33.)

This form may be found in countless instrumental movements written by composers whose maturity fell in the first half of the 18th century, and whose conception of music was mainly contrapuntal. It was often the form of the short dance or other movement which sometimes followed the fugal Allegro in the French *Ouverture*, and may also be the plan of the short second or third movement in the Italian opera *Sinfonia*.

In more extended movements written in this two-part form the central melodic idea may generate one or more complementary ideas or figures which seem to grow-out of it but do not constitute newly conceived themes or melodies intended to contrast with the main idea. Examples of the extended two-part form may be found in the slow movements of the symphonies by Stamitz, Holzbauer and Toëschi,[2] as well as in numerous intrumental movements by J. S. Bach and his contemporaries. Although commonly in three-part form, instances do occur in which either the Minuet or the Trio in Haydn's and Mozart's symphonies is in two-part form.[3] Very similar in style are the movements that are based on one central theme, yet which take the shape of a three-part or *ernary movement. The only difference between this and the two-part form already described is that the first part is now recapitulated with the return of the tonic key after the modulating section, and then, instead of moving away from

---

[1] This qualification will not be repeated, and must be understood in connection with all ref'rences to cadences or themes in the dominant key.
[2] All in E.C.S.   [3] Mozart, Nos. 13, 18, 20; Haydn, Nos. 35, 51, 66.

the tonic to the dominant key as it did in the first part, the music remains in the tonic key; the third part, therefore, amounts to a repetition of the first part with its ending transposed into the tonic key. Just as in the two-part form, complementary melodic ideas may appear during the course of the movement without becoming distinctive enough to be regarded as new or self-contained themes. Examples of the three-part from based on one central theme are to be found in the first and third movements of Arne's Symphony No. 4 in F, in the slow movement of Schwindl's Symphony in F,[1] in the Giga of Arne's overture to *The Judgement of Paris*,[1] and in some of the Minuet's in Handel's overtures.

A larger three-part form is that in which an entirely new and self-contained theme is interposed between the first statement of the main theme and its re-statement or recapitulation. Here the two themes are separate entities, each having its own character and tonality. The larger the scale of the movement, the stronger will be the contrast between the two themes. This form was sometimes used for the second and third movements in the opera *Sinfonia* and in concert-symphonies, and is also the familiar and inevitable form of the Minuet and Trio. In the latter case both the Minuet and the Trio are commonly each in the three-part form described in the last paragraph, as they are in most of Haydn's and Mozart's symphonies:

Minuet	Trio	Minuet
A	B	A
| |	| |	| |
a - b - a	a - b - a	a - b - a

When used for slow movements or short movements, the contrast between the two themes, and their demarcation, is generally less pronounced than in the case of the Minuet and Trio, and the second theme is approached much in the same way as the cadence in the dominant key is reached in the old two-part form. The Aria with *Da Capo* is another familiar example of this three-part form, which is sometimes called Song Form (*Lied-form*) by German theorists.

---
[1] Both in E.C.S.   [2] 18th C.O.

The two and three-part forms of the early 18th century between them provided all the necessary framework for the future Sonata Form. Composers of the generation of Bach and Handel, who thought in terms of contrapuntal movement, used short melodic units to build up a texture in which part-movement provided the main interest, and for which tonality supplied the broad outlines. Their successors, thinking in terms more melodic and harmonic than contrapuntal, sought to maintain the interest by contrasting themes that were built up of four or eight-bars units, and which together formed themselves into separate melodic entities, each of which was self-sufficient and supported by its own harmonic scheme. They also began, in their quite rudimentary way, to make use of orchestral colour to enhance the effect and heighten the contrast between one theme and another.

The second theme, or Second Subject in Sonata Form, was the first outcome of this changing style and new conception. The cadence in the dominant key that marked the end of the first part, and which reappeared transposed into the tonic key at the end of the movement in the old two-part form, contained the germ of the Second Subject which in Sonata Form appeared in the dominant key in the Exposition and subsequently reappeared in the tonic key in the last part as Recapitulation. The mere cadence in the older form was sometimes expanded into a group of four bars, as in the following example by Handel, without introducing any fresh thematic matter:

Ex.1

The cadential bars might be expanded into a much longer group without giving the impression that a new theme is being enunciated, as, for example, in the ten-bar refrain in the first movement of Arne's Symphony in F.[1] But when, the dominant key having been established, the music was halted and, so to speak, took a fresh breath, and then enunciated a theme entirely unrelated to what had preceded it, however short or tentative it might be, the Second Subject was coming into bud, and required only further nourishment and growth to bring it into full flower. Such a rudimentary Second Subject will be found in the first movement of Stamitz's Symphony in G[2] at Letter B (four bars in the dominant) and again at Letter E (four bars in the tonic).

The first movements of *Sinfonias*, overtures, concertos and sonatas written during the 'fifties and 'sixties will provide abundant examples of the Second Subject already established in its own right, and no longer a mere appendage or refrain serving only to round off the main or principal subject of the movement.

The first part or Exposition of a first movement written in the 'fifties or early 'sixties was now planned approximately as follows: a main theme or First Subject, commonly made up of more than one melodic unit, might occupy eight or sixteen bars in the tonic key; a modulation (transition) to the dominant key followed, and established the new tonality in a *tutti* which might continue for another sixteen bars or thereabouts, and usually ended with two or three loud chords. At this point there was a temporary interruption of the continuity of the music, and one which formed the first landmark in the progress of the movement. The new theme, or Second Subject, was then enunciated, and presently merged into another *tutti*, still in the dominant key, which likewise usually ended with a few loud and emphatic chords and was often marked by a double-bar and repeat sign. Here again there was a temporary stoppage, perhaps even more pronounced than the first stoppage.

Just as the second half of the old two-part form often began with the central idea transposed into the dominant key, so the next and corresponding section (Development) of the budding Sonata Form usually started off with the First Subject

---
[1] E.C.S.   [2] E.C.S.

in the dominant key. The same matter was then taken through a few related keys preparatory to making a return to the original key of the movement. In the *Sinfonias* and early concert-symphonies this middle section is often very short, and may be little more than a connecting link, perhaps a sequence or two, without any real thematic development, but which, nevertheless, keeps up the sense of continuity and sooner or later leads back to the tonic key. Without making a re-statement of the opening theme as it was presented at the beginning of the movement, the matter used in the Exposition is resumed more or less at the point where originally it had begun to modulate, but the modulation is now avoided and (transferred into the tonic key) the same matter leads to a restatement of the Second Subject in that key, with possibly a slight extension of the last few bars in a final close which may be regarded as a rudimentary Coda.

This form, which might be called Semi-Sonata Form, required only a longer Development and a return to or Recapitulation of the First Subject to complete the Sonata Form that is commonly found in the first movements and often in the last movements of concert-symphonies written in the later 'sixties and 'seventies. Examples of this immature or Semi-Sonata Form can be seen in the first movements of the symphonies by Stamitz in G, Filtz in E flat, Toëschi in D, Gossec in D, Maldere in B flat, Holzbauer in E flat, J. C. Bach in B flat,[1] in the earliest symphonies of Haydn and Mozart, as well as in numerous similar works by contemporary and less-known composers.

Movements in which the end of the Development is followed by a formal re-statement of the First Subject, just as it had been at the beginning of the movement, were being written before the Semi-Sonata Form was superseded; indeed, both can be found in works that belong to the 'sixties, and both may occur among symphonies written by the same composer. More development of matter derived from the Exposition, some contrapuntal treatment of the figures or melodic units, and occasionally some episodical interpolations, at the same time tended to increase the length and importance of the Development, and gave the whole movement a tripartite form in which the Exposition, Development and Recapitulation

---
[1] All in E.C.S.

were now more evenly proportioned and better balanced. Short Codas of perhaps four or eight bars sometimes rounded off both the Exposition and the Recapitulation, and with that the Sonata Form was complete as far as its design was concerned, but still required a broadening of its outlines and a better integration of the parts that went to make up the whole, before it was fit to serve the ultimate purpose of the two great composers whose works of the 'eighties and 'nineties brought the 18th century symphony to its culminating point.

First movements in this somewhat contracted but structurally complete Sonata Form can be found in almost any quantity among symphonies written in the 'sixties, 'seventies and early 'eighties. The examples by Abel, Schwindl, Dittersdorf,[1] and the overtures in B flat by J. C. Bach and to *The Duenna* by Thomas Linley jun.,[2] are only a handful that might be matched by dozens of others composed by such as Vanhall, Richter, Eichner, Rosetti, Carl Stamitz, Schmittbauer, Cannabich, Pichl, Boccherini and a host of others, most of whose names will be found in the list appended to this book. In the meantime all of these were being outstripped by the rapidly developing young Mozart and the more leisurely progression of the older man, Haydn, and the concert-symphony was now finally breaking away from the old opera *Sinfonia* that had given it birth.

The more leisurely pace of a slow movement necessarily reduces the length, reckoned in bars, of the middle movement of a symphony. For an Italian opera *Sinfonia* or a concert-symphony modelled on the same pattern, from 25 to 50 bars might suffice, unless the bar-value itself were very short, as in the case of 3/8 or 2/4 time. The plans commonly adopted for slow movements in the earlier symphonies were the two-part or three-part forms already described, with the same key-relationship between the parts. This was often expanded after the mid-century into a design which may equally well be regarded as either an extended three-part form or a contracted Sonata Form, viz., A Tonic—B Dominant—A Tonic—B Tonic. A short connecting link between the first B and the second A also occurs, and may expand into a short Development, thus making a Sonata Form in miniature. All of these forms occur in the slow movements of the 'fifties,'sixties

---
[1] E.C.S.   [2] 18th C.O.

and 'seventies, and are found in the earlier Haydn and Mozart symphonies, sometimes with slight divergences which may include the introduction of episodical matter. Haydn often used Variation Form for his slow movements, sometimes with elaborated solo parts for selected instruments.

In the later symphonies the slow movements are more elaborately planned, and may contain more than two themes, more expansion and development of thematic material, and often a strongly contrasted middle section in a minor key.

Something approximating to Rondo Form may also be found in some slow movements, and exceptional types are always liable to crop up, as, for example, a Polonaise which occurs in two of six symphonies by Valentin Nicolay.

The Minuet and trio did not normally form part of the Italian *Sinfonia*, although it may be found displacing the usual final Presto often enough; but it is found in some of the Mannheim four-movement symphonies written before the mid-century, and also in the works of the earlier Viennese group—Monn, Reutter and Wagenseil. The form is, of course, the inevitable A-B-A, the second A being an exact repetition of the first.

Coming after the slow movement, the Minuet and Trio established itself as part of the four-movement symphony from the 'sixties onward. It is rarely absent in Haydn's symphonies after 1764, and is found in most of Mozart's except in the very earliest and in those that are palpably written to conform to the plan of the Italian *Sinfonia*. The expansion of each section beyond the formal eight or sixteen-bar groups, by means of sequences, development or delayed cadences, greatly increased the length of the Minuet and Trio in the later symphonies. By way of curiosities, a Minuet in Rondo Form in one of Abel's symphonies,[1] and a rather novel trumpet Minuet, constructed out of the open notes of the trumpet, in Arne's overture to *Elfrida*, may deserve mention.

The last movements of the earlier opera *Sinfonia* and concert-symphonies were more remarkable for their brevity and levity than for any other quality, the first of these being aggravated by the composer's frequent choice of the shortest possible bar-length (3/8) and the quickest possible speed (Presto). The movements are all in one or other of the forms already

---

[1] Op. X, No. 2.

described, except that Rondo Form occurs more often than in any of the other movements.

In its simplest form the Rondo consists of three statements of a main theme between which are sandwiched two fresh themes or episodes: A-B-A-C-A. The main theme is commonly in the same key each time, but may occasionally make its second appearance in the dominant key, as it does in J. C. Bach's Symphony in B flat.[1] Another form of Rondo uses the same secondary theme twice in place of the two episodes: A-B-A-B-A, and in the later and more highly organised Rondos there is generally some development of thematic matter.

During the 'sixties the last movements were still short and slight, but in the 'seventies they gained length and importance, and the very short bar-length was no longer the rule. Although still active and bustling, the Finale was now shedding the irresponsible gaiety and feverish haste to reach its end as soon as possible that characterised the third movement of the opera *Sinfonia*. With a longer and more substantial last movement, the symphony as a whole was better balanced, and the interest was not allowed to flag nor the work to peter out in an empty-headed little movement that could do no more than frivol for a bare two or three minutes.

Sonata and Rondo are the two forms most commonly used in the last movements of symphonies that date from the 'seventies and 'eighties; other forms occur exceptionally, such as, for example, the Variations in Haydn's No. 31 (Horn Signal), or the Chaconne in a symphony in B flat by Cannabich, and another in a two-movement symphony by Jommelli which, judging by the number of times it was published, must have been very popular in its day.

With the 'eighties we get into the period of Haydn's Paris Symphonies, Mozarts "Prague" (1786), and his three great works in E flat, G minor and C major, which seem to have been created during a few crowded months in the summer of 1788.

In the final movements of his last four symphonies Mozart achieved a level that had never before been reached, and the Finale of his Jupiter symphony—a fugal Sonata Form—remains to this day a phenomenon, a dazzling crown to the

---

[1] B.C.S.

symphony such as had never been approached and was never to be equalled during the 18th century.

A few years later Haydn's London Symphonies yielded a type of Finale that might well be described as the outcome of a marriage between Rondo and Sonata Form. From the Rondo it inherited the periodical reappearances of the main theme, and from Sonata Form the extended thematic developments and the broad outlines of a design that still retained the tripartite division of the movement into Exposition, Development and Recapitulation, now capped (or should it be tailed?) by a longer Coda which was wont to indulge in some caprices of its own.

V

SCORE, PARTS AND ORCHESTRATION

ONCE a composer is admitted into the category of the Great, every effort is made to recover and preserve his autograph scores. Even so, many are lost sight of, and the music is handed down only in copies made by other hands, while many orchestral works survive only in the form of instrumental parts, MS. or printed. Of Haydn's 104 authenticated symphonies, for example, less than half are preserved in autograph scores, some are known only by copied MS. scores, and others only by means of printed parts; and that is the record of a composer whose symphonies were fully appreciated during his lifetime, which when printed were best-sellers, and whose output has been the subject of careful research and collation.

The 18th century composer who failed to qualify as Great, and whose music went out of circulation soon after his death, fared much worse. His immediate successors did not reverently preserve every note written with his own hand, his autograph scores were neglected, lost sight of, scattered, or allowed to perish; even if they survived, they might be difficult to locate and identify. MS. copies were treated with even less respect, and MS. parts were apt to be dealt with as one deals with waste paper. The output of the lesser composer generally goes through a bad time until the music becomes old enough to acquire some antiquarian value, and then it is too late to recover much that has been lost or destroyed.

Engraving and printing music implies a multiplication of copies much greater in number than is ever accomplished by hand-copying. As far as the writer is aware, not a single symphony was printed in score during the 18th century unless it was also the overture to an opera or other work of which the whole or a selection was published in score.[1] Vast quantities of overtures, symphonies and concertos, however, were published in parts (i.e. separate orchestral parts) during the 18th century,[2] and so it happens that a large proportion of 18th century symphonies have survived in no other form than that of printed parts.

To all that have delved amongst the old sets of printed parts that are to be found in many large musical libraries the words that occur on the outside cover with tiresome monotony—Overture or Symphony " in 8 parts " or " *à 8 parties* "—will be very familiar. The eight parts are almost invariably the four string parts and two each for oboes and horns. In the earlier issues the wind parts are *Ad libitum*, but in the later sets they are *Obbligato*. The eight-part set was obviously the standard way of publishing an orchestral work at the minimum cost in engraving and paper. The four string parts were essential, because therein lay practically the whole content of the music. Although early in the century the oboes often ran in unison with the violins, they had always enjoyed a certain amount of independence, and this independence was growing; moreover, when the instrumental style changed about the middle of the century, and the violins were more and more occupied in playing quickly reiterated semiquavers or quavers, a feature of bowed-string technique for which there is no equivalent in wind-instrument technique, the oboe parts had to be modified in order to suit the instrument. The publisher, therefore, could not escape engraving separate oboe parts; he could not, as formerly, make one part do for both oboes and violins.[3] Nor could he avoid engraving separate parts for the horns. At that time the horns had large gaps in their scale, and could not therefore just be directed to play in unison with a string part; a special part had always to be written for the horns and adapted to the limited scale of the valveless instrument.

---

[1] In London it was often only the " Overture and Favourite Songs " that appeared in score. The piano-score was a later method of publishing.
[2] See Appendix A.   [3] This was often done in Handel's overtures.

Ex. 2

But the bassoons, although included in every orchestra and playing in every overture and symphony, were normally occupied in playing the bass part, and no publisher in his senses would have thought of engraving a separate part for bassoons which would have been only a duplication of the general bass part that was used in common by the 'cello and double-bass, and served also for the conductor at the keyboard-instrument. If a few bars were to be played by bassoons alone, they could always be included in the general bass part with some appropriate direction, such as "Fagotti soli," to distinguish them from the rest of the part. This, in fact, was very often done, and little snatches of bassoon parts are to be found in many printed *basso continuo* parts. This in itself is sufficient to prove that bassoons were commonly used to play the bass part although they were not specified in the score. But a separate part for bassoons was uncommon until about the 'eighties, when composers were beginning to treat these instruments as inner harmonists or as melodists in the tenor register; a special part then became a necessity. Up till then, no doubt the bassoon players, as a matter of custom, adapted the parts to suit their instrument, for the bass parts at that time often included long stretches of reiterated quavers[1] or semiquavers, and these, even if playable, would be ineffective on the bassoon, and would almost certainly be played as sustained notes. An old bound book of parts in the writer's possession, containing over sixty overtures, is labelled "Bassoons," but not a single one of these parts is specifically for these instruments; they are all bass parts, variously headed *Basso*, *Basso Continuo*, *Organo* or *Violoncello and Organo*. When the boy Mozart was in London in 1764, he made a copy of the score of a symphony in E flat by C. F. Abel for strings, clarinets, horns and bassoons (K 18); but when the same symphony was published in 1767 as No. 6 of Abel's Op. VII, it was for the usual combination of strings, oboes and horns. Clarinets were not available at that time in most orchestras, so their parts were turned over to the oboes, and any independent matter for the bassoons was embodied in the general bass part called *Basso*, actually the figured bass or *Basso Continuo*.

It was not until round about 1780 that Haydn began regularly to write specific bassoon parts in his symphonies; previous to that only some 16 out of 70 of his symphonies contain any traces of bassoon parts. According to the scores in the *Gesamtausgabe*, Mozart wrote a bassoon part in only two of his symphonies before 1778. There can be no doubt, however, that in these, as well as in hundreds of contemporary symphonies that have survived only in printed parts for strings, oboes and horns, bassoons were used as a matter of course even though no parts specifically for these instruments were ever written.

There is also good reason to suppose that many of these eight-part symphonies included trumpets and drums in their

---

[1] The Germans called it *Trommelbass*, i.e. drum-bass.

original instrumentation. Parts for these instruments were rarely essential, and could be omitted without any loss except of colour and volume, they were, in fact, *Ad libitum* parts. But contemporary MS. sets of parts sometimes contain trumpet and drum parts that are not found in the eight-part printed sets of the same works. The writer has come across instances of this among the symphonies of Stamitz and Pleyel, and no doubt more could be found if old MS. sets and their printed versions were carefully collated. At least four of Haydn's earlier symphonies which in the first four volumes of the *Gesamtausgabe* (Nos. 1 to 49) appear without trumpets and drums, are listed in the Kees Catalogue[1] with parts for these instruments, indeed, the specifications in that catalogue rather suggest that most of Haydn's symphonies written in the 'seventies and 'eighties originally included trumpet and drum parts even if there is no sign of them in the printed sets of parts. Even when some of Haydn's earlier and mid-period symphonies were published for the first time in score by Leduc at Paris in 1801–1806, several trumpet and drum parts were omitted, as, for example, in the *Impériale* (No. 53) and the *Laudon* (No. 69); and when Cianchettini and Sperati produced the first English scores of the same works in 1807–1809, all the trumpet and drum parts were omitted; even the Oxford symphony was without them.

Sometimes a publisher would make a concession and include an essential flute part in the oboe part, or a bassoon part in the bass part, and Bland in London allowed the trumpets to share the same parts with the horns in the *Laudon* Symphony. But on the whole it seems as if trying to get a publisher to engrave an extra part over and above the usual eight was like trying to get blood out of a stone.

A great advance in the manner of orchestrating during the last quarter of the 18th century involved much more independence in the parts written for the wind instruments, and separate parts for each then became almost unavoidable. Some of the later printed sets had to provide the flutes, bassoons, possibly clarinets, each with their own parts, and trumpets and drums could no longer be regarded as entirely *Ad libitum*. The eight parts were then increased to ten, twelve or more, and instead of the old legend "*à 8 parties*"

---

[1] A MS. thematic catalogue of Haydn's symphonies made by or for a Viennese music-lover named Franz Bernhard Ritter von Kees, 1790–1792.

we find such as "*à grand orchestre*" or "*plusieurs instruments.*" But the old eight-part formula died hard, and in the 'eighties and 'nineties such as Pleyel's symphonies were still being issued with no more than oboe and horn parts in addition to the strings, although the full instrumentation included flute, bassoon, trumpet and drum parts.

The full score of a symphony was not commonly used at the actual performance of the work during the 18th century. It had to be written in the first place, it provided the copyist with his material, and it was a convenient way of sending a MS. work from one place to another. But at the performance the keyboard-conductor played from the bass part, often figured for his benefit, and the leader of the violins (the actual controller of the orchestra) had only the first violin part in front of him. These circumstances will account for the complete lack of printed full scores of symphonies in that century; the parts sufficed for a performance—the score was not indispensable. Even for Beethoven's first six symphonies (1801–1809) the parts were all that appeared in print until 1822, when the first authorised scores[1] were published at Bonn and Leipzig.

The orchestration of symphonies, overtures and concertos in the 18th century can be roughly divided into the prevailing styles of three periods. Because of the inevitable overlap of all changes in musical art, these periods can never be defined as beginning in one year and ending in another. It must suffice to say that the first manner of treating the orchestra is that practised by Bach, Handel, and all their contemporaries; the second by the less prominent composers whose symphonies form the main subject for comment in this book, including the early and mid-period works of Haydn and Mozart; the last stage is well exemplified by the orchestration in the last few symphonies of Haydn and Mozart.

In the first period the main interest lies in the part-writing as such, rather than in the colouring that is created by allotting one sort of part to a particular sort of instrument and another sort of part to another sort of instrument. The wood-wind parts are very much the same as those written for the strings, and the brass parts (horns and trumpets) are as much like the string and wood-wind parts as the composers could make them

---

[1] Unauthorised scores of Beethoven's first three symphonies were published in London by Cianchettini and Sperati in 1807–1809.

under the handicap of a limited and incomplete scale of sounds. All instruments therefore get *the same sort of part;* they are virtually interchangeable, subject always to the limitations of the natural brass instruments and the restricted downward compass of the wood-wind. The colour is largely confined to that which is obtainable by contrasting the tone of the string orchestra with that of the double-reeds (oboes and bassoons), and with such passages for brass instruments as could be coaxed out of a scale which provided consecutive notes only in the highest and most unmanageable part of their compass. Almost any instrumental music by Bach or Handel will provide examples of this manner of writing for the orchestra; the overtures of Handel and the Suites of Bach will show how the composers impartially allotted one type of part to three different types of instrument. The overture to Handel's *Esther* and Arne's *The Judgement of Paris*,[1] also the Symphony in F by the latter,[2] show the same process in operation, namely, making the instrument suit the part rather than the part suit the instrument. Nevertheless, Arne's orchestration already presages the coming change; it is, in fact, a halfway house between the old and the new style, as may be seen by comparing the treatment of the strings and wood-wind in the two overtures *Esther* and *The Judgement of Paris.*

To the general ensemble must always be added the sound of the harpsichord that was employed in realizing the harmony implied in the *basso continuo* or universal bass part.

The orchestration of the second period shows the string parts assuming a character which is created out of bowed-instrument technique, while the wood-wind take to a more vocal and sustained type of part. The strings are active, much engaged in playing reiterated semiquavers or quavers, and more occupied with passage-work characteristic of the bowed instrument, with the wood-wind sustaining the harmony in longer notes. The brass parts have largely abandoned any attempt to follow the string parts, and are content to play in their safer and less obtrusive middle register, adding colour, volume, rhythm and cohesion, rather than contributing to the melodic contours of the music. The main contrasts between the reed and the string groups remain as before, but

---
[1] 18th C.O. [2] E.C.S.

the wood-wind also get independent melodic parts that are accompanied by the strings. The general effect is more that of harmonic sonority than of polyphonic movement, and although the parts are often woefully dull in themselves, they certainly did contribute towards the building up of some purely orchestral textures that were the forerunners of 19th century orchestration.

The distribution of the parts, apart from their character, is still very much the same as in the older style. The composers seem to have been always thinking in three parts, and placed the two violin parts close together, often running in thirds or sixths, and appeared to be at a loss to know what to do with the viola.[1] The lay-out of the string parts is very much the same as that in the trio-sonatas for two violins and *basso continuo* that were written in large quantities by the composers of that period, and also in the trio-symphonies[2] often written by Stamitz, his disciples and successors, and which can hardly be distinguished from the trio-sonatas except that they were designed to be played by several players to each part instead of by solo instrumentalists. There is also much labour-saving in the second violin parts; *col violino primo* was so quickly written, and it saved all the trouble of inventing and writing down another part. The 'cellos have next to no independence, and share the *basso continuo* with the double-basses, the bassoon, and the left hand of the keyboard-conductor. But the bass part is obviously thought out in terms of string-technique, and contains (alas!) more than enough of the reiterated "trommelbass," in which the violas usually join for want of anything better to do. It is the texture of the string parts that has changed, but not the lay-out.

As long as the wood-wind were confined to three parts, i.e. two oboes and a bassoon, the lay-out for these instruments is necessarily thin, and in fact, very similar to that of the strings in that the two upper parts are widely separated from their bass. But the more consistent use of wood-wind for sustaining the harmony, for accompanied solo melodies, and for independent counter-melodies is all to the good, and looks forward rather than backward. There is a certain free-and-easy exchange of wood-wind instruments, at any rate in the printed parts—flutes *or* oboes, oboes *or* clarinets—but one

---

[1] Berlioz was right when he wrote: "the majority of the composers of the last century rarely writing four real parts, scarcely knew what to do with it"; i.e. the viola. (*Instrumentation*, Eng. tr., p. 25.)

[2] Called Orchestra Trios by the English publishers.

suspects that this was a publisher's proviso calculated to help the sale of the parts. It would have been bad business to insist on clarinets as long as these instruments were to be found only in a few of the largest orchestras. The rather uneventful horn parts keep to the open notes, and only in special solo parts[1] is any virtuosity expected, or any display of the hand-technique. But these rather dull horn parts did give body to the middle of the lay-out just where it was very sparsely provided with sounds, while the trumpets and drums contribute colour, volume and brightness to the loud *tuttis*.

The foregoing remarks apply to the orchestration of the crowd of composers who wrote large quantities of symphonies in the 'fifties, 'sixties and 'seventies, and to a certain extent to the works of Haydn and Mozart that belong to the same period. But the inborn musicianship of the two greater composers shows itself in their handling of the orchestra even in their earlier works, and especially in the better lay-out of their string parts. The very quality of the music seems to carry with it a better conception of how to distribute the parts and colour the orchestration, even though there is much in it that savours of the past. Mozart especially, showed a sense for orchestral effect that in the 'seventies ran well ahead of anything that the older man Haydn could show him; but neither could help giving their scores a finish which, however antiquated the style might be, always stamped them with the hall-mark of superior workmanship.

In the orchestration of the last two decades of the 18th century it becomes obvious that the keyboard-conductor was, so to speak, being warned that his services would soon no longer be required. Although he clung to his office for many years more, both he and his function were doomed eventually to become extinct. The lay-out of the parts show that little account was now being taken of the right hand harpsichord or piano chords that were formerly deemed indispensable to the harmony and sonority of the orchestral ensemble. Although 18th century composers never completely threw off the habit of thinking in three parts for strings, the inner harmony is now better provided for by more useful viola parts, and also by a more general use of a pair of bassoons in the tenor register. The one-time emptiness in

---

[1] See the horn parts in Haydn, No. 31 and No. 51, Adagio.

18th CENTURY SYMPHONIES 49

the middle of the harmony gives place to a lay-out which better nourishes the inside of the chord, or, in plainer words, gives it more notes. The discovery that the 'cello possessed valuable qualities as a melodist in the tenor register also adds to the fullness and interest of the sound of the string orchestra.

The wood-wind group was now expanding. The day when a pair of oboe notes, separated by a wide gulf from a bassoon note, sufficed for the wood-wind harmony was nearly over. Independent flute parts were already creeping in during the 'seventies, and with two bassoon parts, now made a five or six-part group of what had formerly been a rather tenuous three-part group. Clarinets were also pressing their claim to be admitted into the group, and when after some hesitation these instruments were *added* to the family, and were no longer only *substituted* for the oboes, the wood-wind group found itself well provided with sounds spread over a wider area, and also with a variety of colour at its disposal that opened out possibilities never dreamed of by the earlier 18th century composers.

The horn parts remained much as they had been, but with an increased tendency to exploit the melodic possibilities of the consecutive part of their scale from the 8th to the 12th open notes, and with some more appreciation of their particular tone-quality. The horns were no longer turned on only to augment the volume of sound in the orchestral *tutti*. Trumpet and drum parts were now being written habitually instead of only occasionally. What they contributed was rarely an indispensable part of the music, but they were valued for their volume-contributing quality and for the brilliance and incisiveness of their tone. Although it is always rash to assert that anything was *never* done, as far as the writer is aware, trombones were not employed in any 18th century symphony, although they were sometimes used in the opera overtures of the 'eighties and 'nineties.

The effect of late 18th century orchestration can be heard almost any day in concert or wireless performances of Haydn's and Mozart's last few symphonies. It is familiar ground and its clarity is such that it requires little or no explanation. Every part is intended to be heard; it is largely self-balancing, unless played with too large a string orchestra; and if it fails in either or both of these respects, the fault lies in the performance.

Of the symphonies written by composers who "also ran" during the last two decades of the 18th century we hear little enough, indeed, we hear hardly anything at all. But one symphony in C by Pleyel[1] has recently been exhumed, and may show that it was not only in the hands of Haydn and Mozart that orchestration was developing and preparing the way for Beethoven, Schubert, Mendelssohn, and the succession of 19th century composers who were going to make the symphony a much more weighty and solemn affair than it had ever been in the 18th century.

---
[1] E.C.S.

VI

ANALYSIS
of the Form of the movements in the two Series
EARLY CLASSICAL SYMPHONIES
and
18TH CENTURY OVERTURES

EARLY CLASSICAL SYMPHONIES

THOMAS AUGUSTINE ARNE—SYMPHONY (OVERTURE) NO. 4 IN F. (1740)

French *Ouverture* with Minuet

I. *Slow introduction* expanded into a movement in three-part form based on one theme. Part one: 20 bars; part two: 8 bars; part three: 14 bars. Part one ends with a ten-bar refrain in the dominant key which is repeated in the tonic key to conclude the movement. Total, 42 bars.

II. *Fugal Allegro.* Three entries of the two-bar Subject with Codetta: 8 bars; Letter A, two entries in the dominant key: 4 bars; episode based on the figure in the Codetta: 7 bars; Letter B, entries, partial and complete, in dominant key: 4 bars; two entries in stretto in tonic key extended by figures to Letter C: 5 bars; Letter C, entries in F (partial), D minor and A minor, extended by figure to Letter D: 9 bars; Letter D, episode based on figure from the Codetta: 4 bars; a fresh episode: 4 bars; Letter E, two entries in subdominant key: 4 bars; episode: 6 bars; Letter F, partial and complete entries in tonic key: 10 bars. Total, 65 bars.

III. *Minuet* (Andantino). Three-part form based on one theme. Part one: 16 bars; part two: 12 bars; part three (Letter B): 12 bars. Total, 40 bars.

JOHANN STAMITZ—SYMPHONY IN G, OP. 3, NO. 3

I. *Semi-Sonata form.* Three introductory bars; main theme, bar 4 to Letter A: 13 bars; Letter A, Transition: 16 bars; Letter B, tentative Second Subject in dominant key with concluding *tutti*: 11 bars; Development: 18 bars; Letter D, transition transposed and reduced: 12 bars;

Letter E, Second Subject in tonic key with concluding *tutti*: 11 bars. Total, 81 bars.

II. *Two-part form based on one theme.* First part: 23 bars; Second part, with episode at Letter C: 27 bars; a refrain of 8 bars concludes each part. Total, 50 bars.

III. *Semi-Sonata form.* First Subject and Transition: 23 bars; Letter B, Second Subject in dominant, arising out of First Subject: 22 bars; Letter D, Development: 25 bars; Transition picked up at Letter F: 7 bars; Letter G, Second Subject in tonic key, with concluding *tutti*: 30 bars. Total, 107 bars.

ANTON FILTZ—SYMPHONY IN E FLAT.

I. *Semi-Sonata form.* First Subject and Transition: 28 bars; Letter B, Second Subject in dominant with concluding *tutti*: 30 bars; Development: 51 bars; return to tonic key at Letter G, and transition picked up at 6 bars before Letter H (see Letter A): 18 bars; Letter H, Second Subject in tonic key with concluding *tutti*: 20 bars. Total, 147 bars.

II. *Miniature Semi-Sonata form* (A-B-Link-Episode-B). First theme with modulation to dominant: 10 bars; Letter A, Second theme in dominant: 13 bars; Letter B, sequential link, episode at Letter C in tonic key: 19 bars; Letter D, Second theme in tonic key: 14 bars. Total, 56 bars.

III. *Semi-Sonata form.* First Subject and Transition: 31 bars; Letter A, Second Subject in dominant, with concluding *tutti*: 38 bars; Letter C, there is no actual Development, but at Letter D the Transition is picked up (see 13th bar from the beginning of the movement) and leads to recapitulation of Second Subject: 52 bars; Letter F, Second Subject in tonic key, with concluding *tutti*, all of which is a transposition of the 38 bars before the double bar: 38 bars. Total, 159 bars.

FRANÇOIS JOSEPH GOSSEC—SYMPHONY IN D

I. *Semi-Sonata form.* Twofold First Subject (bar 1 and bar 12) and Transition: 43 bars; Letter B, Second Subject in dominant, and an additional idea at Letter C: 38 bars; Letter D, short Development: 24 bars; Letter E, recapitulation of second part of First Subject and Transition as before: 32 bars; Letter G, Second Subject in tonic: 15 bars; Letter H, Coda, including the idea first introduced at Letter C: 30 bars. Total, 182 bars.

II. *A-B-A-B.* Twofold First Subject: 19 bars; Letter B, twofold Second Subject (ten and seven-bar themes) in relative major key with Coda (7 bars): 30 bars; Letter D, First Subject in relative major key, but returning to tonic minor key: 22 bars; Letter E, Second Subject and Coda in tonic minor key: 31 bars. Total, 102 bars.

III. *Semi-Sonata form.* First Subject and Transition: 53 bars; Letter B, Second Subject in dominant: 55 bars; Coda: 27 bars; Letter F, Development: 59 bars; Letter H, Second Subject and Coda in tonic key: 112 bars. Total, 306 bars.

PIERRE VAN MALDERE—SYMPHONY IN B FLAT

I. *Semi-Sonata form.* First Subject and Transition with a secondary idea of thematic importance at Letter A: 41 bars; Letter B, Second Subject in dominant, returning to the secondary idea at Letter D: 47 bars; Development: 48 bars; Letter H, Recapitulation of the secondary idea in tonic key: 19 bars; Letter I, Second Subject in tonic key with secondary idea as Coda: 41 bars. Total, 196 bars.

II. *Semi-Sonata form.* Twofold First Subject: 10 bars; Letter A, Second Subject in relative major: 17 bars; Letter C, Development: 13 bars; Letter E, recapitulation of second part of First Subject, followed by Second Subject in tonic minor key: 19 bars. Total, 59 bars.

III. *Semi-Sonata form.* First Subject and Transition: 32 bars; Letter B, First Subject in dominant key followed by Coda (at Letter C): 32 bars; Development with episode at 12th bar after Letter E: 60 bars; Letter F, return to tonic key, followed by First Subject in tonic key and Coda: 42 bars. The First Subject also serves as the Second Subject. Total, 166 bars.

IGNAZ HOLZBAUER—SYMPHONY IN E FLAT

I. *Semi-Sonata form.* First Subject and Transition: 16 bars; Letter A, Second Subject in the dominant, followed by another at Letter B, and Coda at Letter C: 32 bars; Development, with episode at Letter D based on first Second Subject: 19 bars; Letter E, recapitulation of second Second Subject in tonic key, part of First Subject, and Coda at Letter G: 35 bars. Total, 102 bars.

II. *Two-part form with a secondary theme.* First part ends at Letter A in relative major key, but a secondary theme has been introduced at the 5th bar from the beginning: 9 bars; Second part begins after a short Coda at Letter A with secondary theme in tonic minor, and concludes with short Coda on a half close: 12 bars. Total, 21 bars.

III. *Minuet and Trio form.* Minuet in three-part form (8-8-8): 24 bars; Trio in two-part form (10–18), the refrain in the dominant at bar 5 is repreated in the tonic at 6 bars from the end: 28 bars; Minuet *Da Capo*. Total, with *Da Capo*, 76 bars.

IV. *Semi-Sonata form.* Multiple first Subject and Transition: 36 bars; Letter C, Second Subject in dominant key, leading to an episode: 14 bars; Letter D, Development begins with the episode of 9 bars in C minor, and leads back to the tonic major key: 32 bars; Letter G, recapitulation of Second Subject in tonic key, followed by matter from the Transition and Coda (Letter I) based on the beginning (bar 5): 38 bars. Total, 120 bars.

CARLO GIUSEPPE TOËSCHI—SYMPHONY IN D

I. *Semi-Sonata form.* First Subject and Transition: 17 bars; Second Subject in dominant: 26 bars; Development with episode at 5th bar after Letter C: 32 bars; Transition is picked up at 4 bars before Letter E, followed by Second Subject in tonic key at Letter E: 30 bars. Total, 105 bars.

II. *Two-part form.* First part ends at Letter B in dominant: 28 bars; Second part: 44 bars. Total, 72 bars.

III. *Sonata form.* First Subject and Transition: 49 bars; Letter C, Second Subject in dominant key and Coda at Letter E: 40 bars; Letter F, Development: 61 bars; Letter I, Recapitulation of First Subject and Second Subject (Letter J) in tonic key with Coda at Letter L: 64 bars. Total, 214 bars.

JOHANN CHRISTIAN BACH—SYMPHONY IN B FLAT, OP. 21, No. 3

I. *Semi-Sonata form.* First Subject and Transition: 24 bars; Letter B, Second Subject in dominant: 25 bars; Letter E, Development starting with First Subject in tonic key (!), link at 7 bars before Letter C: 30 bars; Letter G, Second Subject in dominant key (!) and conclusion in tonic key: 28 bars. Total, 107 bars.

Alternatively: A-B-A-B. A: from beginning to Letter B; B: from Letter B to Letter E; A: Letter E to Letter G; B: Letter G to the end.

II. *Three-part form.* First theme and modulation: 22 bars; Letter B, Second theme in dominant: 16 bars; Letter D, First theme and Coda: 20 bars. Total, 58 bars.

III. *Rondo.* Main theme ends at Letter A: 16 bars; Letter A, First episode: 8 bars; Main theme in dominant key: 8 bars; Letter B, Second episode: 16 bars; Main theme in tonic key: 19 bars. Total, 67 bars.

CARL FRIEDRICH ABEL—SYMPHONY IN E FLAT, OP. 10, NO. 3

I. *Sonata form.* First Subject and Transition: 32 bars; Letter B, Second Subject in dominant and concluding *tutti*: 30 bars; Letter D, Development, beginning with an episode and ending with a modulating link: 48 bars; Letter G, Recapitulation of First Subject, followed by Second Subject (Letter I) in tonic key and concluding *tutti*: 64 bars. Total, 174 bars.

II. *Miniature Sonata form.* First theme: 10 bars; Letter A, Second theme: 12 bars; Letter B, Development: 14 bars; Letter C, Recapitulation of First theme followed by Second theme (Letter D) in tonic key : 22 bars. Total, 48 bars.

III. *Rondo.* Main theme: 16 bars; Episode in dominant key: 8 bars; Letter A, main theme in dominant key: 8 bars; Episode: 8 bars; Letter B, main theme in tonic key: 16 bars; Letter C, Coda and main theme to conclude: 20 bars. Total, 76 bars.

C. FRIEDRICH SCHWINDL—SYMPHONY IN F

I. *Sonata form.* First Subject and Transition: 28 bars; Letter B, Second Subject in dominant, with *tutti* and Coda (5 bars): 28 bars; Letter D, Development: 34 bars; Letter F, Recapitulation of First Subject, Second Subject in tonic key (Letter H) and Coda: 56 bars. Total, 146 bars.

II. *Three-part form based on one idea.* First part and modulation to dominant key: 28 bars; modulating middle part: 38 bars; Letter F, First part, remaining in tonic key, with Coda (Letter G): 22 bars. Total, 88 bars.

III. *Sonata form.* First Subject and Transition: 18 bars; Second Subject in dominant with Coda (Letter B): 23 bars; Development: 22 bars; Letter D, Recapitulation of First

Subject and Second Subject in tonic key, with Coda: 43 bars. Total, 106 bars.

CARL VON DITTERSDORF—SYMPHONY IN C

I. *Sonata form.* First Subject: 22 bars; Letter A, Second Subject in dominant key and continuation based on second part of First Subject: 41 bars; Development: 32 bars; Recapitulation, without Second Subject: 32 bars. Total, 127 bars.

II. *Miniature Sonata form.* First theme and modulation: 12 bars; Second theme in dominant: 12 bars; Letter B, link or Development: 8 bars; Letter C, First theme: 8 bars; Letter D, Second theme in tonic key: 8 bars; Coda: 12 bars. Total, 60 bars.

III. *Sonata form with only one Subject.* Main Subject and *tutti*: 24 bars; Letter B, main Subject in dominant key, with *tutti* and Coda (Letter C): 31 bars; Letter D, Development: 22 bars; Recapitulation of main Subject (7th bar after Letter E), with *tutti*: 24 bars; Letter G, main Subject in tonic key (as at Letter B in dominant) with *tutti* and Coda: 31 bars. Total, 132 bars.

IGNAZ JOSEPH PLEYEL—SYMPHONY IN C

I. Slow introduction in C minor: 25 bars; Allegro molto (*Sonata form*), First Subject and Transition: 29 bars; Second Subject in dominant key, with *tutti*: 78 bars; Development: 54 bars; Recapitulation (the join is concealed): 31 bars; Second Subject in tonic key: 49 bars; First Subject as Coda: 13 bars. Total, 254 bars.

II. *A-Episode-B-A-B.* First theme and modulating link: 21 bars; Episode in dominant key: 14 bars; modulating section: 8 bars; Second theme in dominant key with Coda: 11 bars; First theme and continuation: 26 bars; Second theme in tonic key with Coda: 17 bars. Total, 97 bars.

III. *Minuet and Trio form.* Minuet in three-part form, with Coda: 10–22–16 bars; Trio in three-part form: 8–8–8 bars; Minuet *Da Capo.* Total, with *Da Capo*, 120 bars.

IV. *Sonata form.* First Subject and Transition: 28 bars; Second Subject in dominant key: 33 bars; Coda and *tutti*: 37 bars; Development: 74 bars; Recapitulation of First Subject: 33 bars; Second Subject in tonic key: 22 bars; Coda: 47 bars. Total, 274 bars.

18th CENTURY OVERTURES

G. F. HANDEL—OVERTURE TO "ESTHER" (1720)

French *Ouverture* with Minuet

I. *Slow Introduction, expanded into a movement in three-part form based on one idea.* First part, ending in dominant key: $8\frac{1}{2}$ bars; second part: $8\frac{1}{2}$ bars; Letter B, third part, ending with a half-close: 9 bars. Total, 26 bars.

II. *Three-part form with two themes.* First theme: 25 bars; Letter D, Second theme: 23 bars; return of First theme: 8 bars. Total, 56 bars.

III. *Fugal Allegro.* First entry of Subject with counterpoint below: $4\frac{1}{2}$ bars; Second entry (Answer), inverted and extended to 6 bars; Third entry in bass, and extended to $7\frac{1}{2}$ bars; Letter H, episode: $8\frac{1}{2}$ bars; entry by second violin, extended to $7\frac{1}{2}$ bars; Letter H, episode: $8\frac{1}{2}$ bars; entry by second violin, extended to $7\frac{1}{2}$ bars; Letter J, partial entries (oboes and bassoon) 6 bars; Letter K, episode: 7 bars; fragments of Subject: $4\frac{1}{2}$ bars; incomplete entries, viola and basses (inverted), extended to 9 bars; entries in stretto: $7\frac{1}{2}$ bars. Total, 68 bars.

THOMAS AUGUSTINE ARNE—OVERTURE TO "THE JUDGEMENT OF PARIS" (1740)

French *Ouverture* with Minuet

I. *Slow introduction*: 22 bars.

II. *Fugal Allegro.* Subject with invertible countersubject, and answer: 11 bars; Letter B, part of Subject and countersubject, extended to $7\frac{1}{2}$ bars; episode: $5\frac{1}{2}$ bars; Letter C, beginnings of Subject in stretto and part of countersubject: 9 bars; (one bar after Letter D) beginnings of Subject in stretto, followed by countersubject in basses: 4 bars; (one bar after Letter F) part of Subject in stretto, followed by part of countersubject in basses, and concluding cadence: 13 bars. Total, 64 bars.

III. *Minuet in three-part form based on one idea.* 16–16–12 bars. Total, 44 bars.

IV. *Gigue in three-part form based on one idea.* 9–12–9 bars. Total, 30 bars.

J. C. BACH—OVERTURE IN B FLAT

Sonata form. First Subject and Transition: 32 bars; Letter B, Second Subject in dominant key, Coda at Letter C:

35 bars; Letter D, Development: 43 bars; Letter G, Recapitulation, First Subject followed by Second Subject in tonic key at Letter H, Coda at Letter I: 63 bars. Total, 173 bars.

ANDRÉ ERNEST MODESTE GRÉTRY—OVERTURE TO " LUCILE " (1769)

Sonata form interrupted by a slow movement; a plan similar to that of Mozart's overture to *Die Entführung aus dem Serail* (1782). First Subject: 29 bars; Letter B, Second Subject in dominant: 22 bars; Letter C, episode: 22 bars; Letter D, First Subject and Coda at Letter F: 39 bars; Andante in three-part form: 14–10–13 bars; return of Vivace with First Subject: 18 bars; 6th bar after Letter I, Second Subject in tonic key and concluding chords: 30 bars. Totals, 112, 37 and 48 bars.

THOMAS LINLEY JUN.—OVERTURE TO " THE DUENNA " (1775)
A three-movement *Sinfonia*

I. First Subject and Transition to A major and E minor: 23 bars; Letter B, Development with episodes: 33 bars; Letter D, First Subject and conclusion: 19 bars. Total, 75 bars.

II. *Three-part form.* 8–8–8 bars. Total, 24 bars.

III. *Rondo, A-B-A-C-B-A-B-A.* Theme in three-part form: 16–8–8 bars; Letter H, episodical Development: 36 bars; Letter K, First theme recapitulated, and Coda: 16–8–18 bars. Total, 110 bars.

PHILIDOR (FRANÇOIS ANDRÉ DANICAN)—OVERTURE TO " LES FEMMES VÉENGES " (1775)

Sonata form with subjects in reversed order in the Recapitulation. First Subject and Transition: 33 bars; Letter B, Second Subject in dominant: 33 bars; Development with new themes at Letters D and E: 56 bars; Letter G, Second Subject in tonic key: 33 bars; Letter I, Recapitulation of First Subject followed by both themes (Letters J and K) from the Development, and concluding *tutti*: 55 bars. Total, 210 bars.

DOMENICO CIMAROSA—OVERTURE TO " THE IMPRESARIO " (1786)

Principal theme and *tutti* modulating to dominant key: 38 bars; Letter B, a second theme in tonic key, with *tutti*:

27 bars; Letter D, link leading to a brief Development at Letter E: 14-19 bars; *tutti* in tonic key and link: 19 bars: leading to principal theme (9th bar after Letter G) and Coda; 44 bars. Total, 161 bars.

VII

CONCLUSION

SYMPHONIES in the 18th century were written to please, and to please at first hearing. Their beauties, even if they were sometimes only skin-deep, were made manifest without calling for any effort on the part of the listener, or for any intensive search. The composer at that time who wrote music that required to be heard several times and the score closely studied before it could be understood, or in which the beauties were so securely hidden that one might be inclined to suspect that there were none, would have been dismissed as incompetent and forced to occupy himself in some other way. The 18th century symphony had to place all its cards on the table face upwards, put all its goods in the shop window, and stand or fall by what it sounded like when it was first heard. There was in it no deep philosophy and no abstruse meaning was carefully tucked away out of sight and hearing in its transparent little score; it required no explaining, no interpretation of any underlying truth, and nothing that only the elect and those blessed with the most penetrating vision could discern in order to fully appreciate its message.

Even in its highest manifestation, as in the three last symphonies of Mozart, the 18th century symphony was intended to give pleasure and entertainment to those who heard it. It may be that Mozart's G minor symphony reveals a " struggle of exalted passion," that it has a " tragic grandeur " that " tears so powerfully at our heart-strings "; it may be that the Minuet tells of a " bitter and merciless struggle "; that the Finale releases a " contorted, demoniac force," a " passionate feverishness," a " poroxsysm of exaltation " like a " raging torrent " that has " burst its banks, uprooting trees and upheaving boulders ";[1] but all these things, and a great deal more that has been attributed to this symphony by gushing 19th and 20th century admirers, were nevertheless expressed by the composer in music that is most pleasant to listen to,

---

[1] aint-Foix, *The Symphonies of Mozart*, Chap. 14.

and that gives as much pleasure to its hearers as the composer's most sprightly Presto or graceful Andante. Even if the last movement of the Jupiter symphony invites more concentrated attention from the listener because of its fugal nature, it can be heard with pleasure by those who know and care nothing about real or tonal answers, invertible countersubjects, stretti, episodes, and all the rest of the terminology of the textbook.

Nor does Haydn's *Trauersymphonie* really tear at our heart-strings very much; on the other hand, it laments in a manner that is easily consolable. After some bars in E minor the music breaks into a jolly *tutti* in the relative major key, and remembers to mourn again only when the original minor key is resumed. The Adagio is as sunny and contented as Haydn's slow movements usually are, and the Finale does not harrow our feelings by the intensity of its grief. It is " Mourning without Tears," and just as enjoyable as any other of the composer's symphonies composed at that time. The solemn introduction to Haydn's last symphony does not delude us into supposing that we are going to hear a tale of heavy tragedy, for we can depend on it, that as soon as the double bar lines are passed the music will break into a smile, and that the trouble portended in the introduction will be forgotten.

The *Tempesta del Mare* in Holzbauer's E flat symphony[1] does not strike terror into our heats, nor do the stormy scale-passages alarm us; the little squirts of demisemiquavers, if they are intended to represent lightning flashes, do not frighten us any more than the red fire of the Demon King in the pantomime. Dittersdorf's symphonies on Ovid's *Metamorphoses* propound no philosophy too deep for human understanding, and do not represent the great Roman poet's work in terms of anything but mildly pleasant music, which indeed was all that the composer of the merry comic opera *Doktor und Apotheker* had it in him to conceive.

The 18th century symphony stuck to its job of providing pleasure and entertainment, and if its emptiness may sometimes strike our sophisticated ears as being a little bit tiresome, we know that it will last for only twenty-five minutes or less.

[1] E.C.S.

18th CENTURY SYMPHONIES

The little ten, fifteen, or twenty-minute symphony of the 'sixties and 'seventies cantered through its first movement with some show of energy and importance; it ambled through its slow movement gracefully and amiably; it went all countrified and bucolic in its Minuet, and danced gaily through its final Presto without stopping to enquire into the why and wherefore of the Eternal Verities. It was a lightly-built stripling, and nobody at that time could have foreseen that it was destined to develop by the beginning of the 20th century into a ponderous heavyweight that demanded an orchestra of a hundred performers and fifty minutes or more to play it.[1]

The 18th century symphonist made it his business to adapt his work to suit the taste of the particular audience for which he was writing; he knew on which side his bread was buttered and, his aim being to please his audience, he tried to give them the sort of thing they liked, in fact, he was much in the same position as the tradesman who knows his customers' tastes, and stocks his shop with the goods he knows they will like and will buy. When Mozart heard that the Paris audiences liked a symphony to begin with a forcible unison passage[2] (*le premier coup d'archet*), he took good care that his work written for the *Concert Spirituel* should begin in that way, and when he learned that the Andante was not quite to their taste, he immediately wrote another one. When in Italy he wrote symphonies as the Italians liked them, on the lines of the opera *Sinfonia*, and at Salzburg he made them conform to the requirements of the Archbishop and his court. When Haydn came to London he adapted some of his symphonies to suit the English taste, and if that taste is reflected in the symphonies he wrote while he was in London, as no doubt it is, we may flatter ourselves that there was nothing much wrong with it.

If we pick the 18th century symphony to pieces and examine the strands which when woven together constitute the material from which it is made, we will find that these elements were all contained in a common source from which any composer was free to help himself. The little clusters of notes, figures, rhythmical patterns, and all the elemental ingredients of the music were not created by any composer in particular, and

---
[1] Bruckner, Mahler, Elgar.
[2] See the beginning of Mozart's Paris Symphony (No. 31), and the beginning of Gossec's Symphony in D (E.C.S.).

18th CENTURY SYMPHONIES

certainly not by Haydn and Mozart; they were generated by some spontaneous process which operates of its own accord wherever and whenever music is made, and forms recognisable entities out of musical atoms that are measurable by pitch and time.

Almost anything would do to start a symphony; a few chords, a scale, a well-worn figure, or more often than not a mere arpeggio on the common chord followed by an afterphrase consisting of a two-part motif in thirds or sixths over a pedal of repeated notes:

The invention or selection of thematic matter does not appear to have given the composers much trouble or concern. The best of them were quite content to use the same or the same sort of material that had already served the purpose of the lesser talents. They all thought in terms of harmony; a chord or a succession of chords underlies every melodic idea, large or small, and whether it is harmonically or contrapuntally presented. His innate musical gift would enable one composer to put together a better melody than another, and his instinctive and superior musicianship would weave the ingredients into a better texture, but the elemental matter he used was the common property of all composers, good, bad and indifferent, and it was just the way he handled these ingredients and the use he put them to that distinguished the quality of the music by one composer from that by another.

Any musical child might have improvised at the piano the naïve tune that Haydn used as the theme for the Andante of his " Surprise " symphony (a), and it required no genius to devise the puerile decoration of the same theme by repeating each note four times (b) :

Ex. 4

Yet, Hadyn could and did make a delightful movement out of this childish conception, but it makes one shudder to think how it would have fared in the hands of a weaker composer.

The methods by which a theme for a first movement was constructed were all in common use by the time Haydn and Mozart began to write symphonies, and only in their later works were these two composers able to evolve the more highly organised type of theme that is found, for example, in the first Allegro (14 bars) of Mozart's E flat symphony (No. 39) and in the Finale (17 bars) of Haydn's Drumroll symphony (No. 103). In general, an eight or sixteen-bar group contained all that was necessary to set forth the whole idea, and it was suually presented for the first time with no more than its accompanying harmony. A device which is exemplified in the beginning of Abel's symphony in G, Op. VII (quoted in Example III) was in constant use by all composers, great and small. Some melodic unit of a bar or two in length would be started by the first violins, and then be taken up by the second violins, while the first violins continued it a third higher; or the process might be reversed in sixths instead of thirds.[1]

While it would be difficult to find a precedent for some of the harmonic progressions employed by Haydn and Mozart in their later symphonies, it would be equally difficult to find a melodic figure or device in the works of these two masters that had not already been used by the composers of the preceding generation. The typically Italian figure shown in the next example, and so freely adopted by Mozart, is one of many that may be found in scores of works written by all manner of composers both before and during his time:

Ex. 5

It was only after the theme had been stated that the real quality of the composer began to emerge. The good composer would manage to make a good movement, marked with his own imprint, out of the same sort of material, used in the same way, from which the lesser man would make a commonplace movement that might have been written by anybody. The two themes in the next Example were written, one by a great composer in 1782, the other by a composer whose name cannot be found in any of our standard Musical Dictionaries,

---

[1] Mozart, No. 28, bars 3 to 6.

the dates of whose birth and death are unrecorded, of whose life nothing is known except that he lived in the second half of the 18th century, and of whom it is safe to assert that not a note of his music has been heard for about 150 years. Both ideas are similar in character, their melodic outlines, although not identical, are strongly akin, they share the same rhythmical plan and are given the same treatment. As regards intrinsic quality, there is not much to choose between them; yet one was wrought into a fine work that is still constantly heard in our concert-rooms, and the other was the theme of a commonplace little Finale in a symphony which, if it ever lived at all, only flickered weakly and then faded out:

When the main theme has been stated the weaker composer can do no more than fill up the space between the two subjects, while the stronger will make the matter grow and advance with purpose towards the point where the next theme is to make its appearance. But it is more particularly in the Development of a symphony that the quality of a composer's work as well as his technical proficiency are put to the test. The smaller man transposes his themes, but does not develop them; he connects them by obvious links and makes his matter hang together by patching it; the greater man exploits his themes, presents them in different aspects, and weaves them into a continuous whole that does not stop to take breath and look around for something to do. It was in the Development that some display of contrapuntal skill was expected; the little man shirks this responsibility and drifts through a few related keys until he thinks he has drifted long enough and is glad to return to the home key. The big man faces his task and builds up a texture of thematic strands that coalesce and keep the music alive with movement while he is guiding it through a cycle of keys that will lead to the Recapitulation. The poor Development is stuck together, and all the joints are exposed; the good Development, however much its aspects change, is all of one piece and does not sag or halt in its progress through the transformations and tonalities that carry it forward to its ultimate goal.

There are plenty of undeveloped Developments in the little symphonies of the 'sixties and 'seventies. In this respect Haydn was undoubtedly in advance of all others, and Mozart only began to catch up with him in his Paris symphony (1778). By the 'eighties the Development could no longer be shirked; a few sequential repetitions and transpositions were not strong enough to balance a structure that was growing more weighty at both ends and called for greater substance in the middle of the movement. Alas! few composers could bear the strain, and many that attempted it could only sustain their efforts by leaning against and imitating the two in whose hands the symphony was left to complete that stage of its growth at which Beethoven and Schubert found it.

But the work of the smaller men was not wasted; indeed, it had provided the necessary foundation, the framework, the tools, the material, the conditions and the circumstances that were essential to the building up of a structure that no one or two men could have created alone and unassisted. The great mound of forgotten symphonies that the 18th century produced may contain a mass of dead music, but it was out of these remains that the last three of Mozart's and the last twelve of Haydn's symphonies drew the nourishment and the stamina that have kept them alive to this day.

If it is to be heard as it was conceived, and balanced as the composer imagined it, an 18th century symphony should be performed by a small orchestra in which the sound of the stringed instruments does not outweigh that of the slender wood-wind group when both are playing together. The rich tone of a large string orchestra, beautiful as it is, only too easily smothers the thin tone of half-a-dozen wood-wind instruments, and easily obscures matter that was intended to stand out clearly and assert itself on equal terms with the string tone. The large concert-halls of the present time, however, require large orchestras, and the increased number of string players to each part that is now customary produces a disequilibrium that is apt to misrepresent the composer's conception and mislead the listener. If we are to hear all the parts in their right proportion, a string orchestra of from 12 to 22 players is all that the few singly represented wood-wind parts can stand up to, however carefully the tone of the former is modified or suppressed. A huge volume of sound is out of keeping with the spirit and style of music that is so sparely built as the 18th century symphony always is. The solution of the problem can be found only in employing small orchestras in small concert-halls, so that the balance that is implicit in the scoring of the works may be restored and the music presented in the spirit in which it was conceived and as far as possible under the conditions that prevailed when it was written.

The old sets of parts rarely contain a duplicate part except that of the bass, which is usually represented by two copies. One of these stood on the harpsichord or piano of the "conductor," and from that same copy one 'cellist and one double-bass player, seated on either side of the conductor, played their part;[1] the other bass part was handed to the

[1] This arrangement is shown in all plans of 18th century orchestras that have survived

bassoon player. These sets of parts were obviously used by small orchestras with not more than two or three first violins and a total force of from 12 to 18 players. La Pouplinières orchestra (1731–1762) comprised five violins, one 'cello, one flute, one oboe, two clarinets, one bassoon, two horns, one clavecin, 1 harp; most of the players were double-handed, and one of the horn players also played the double-bass.[1] That was the sort of orchestra for which the earlier 18th century symphonies were designed—a total force of 15 players!

But such were the chamber orchestras of the 18th century when the term " chamber music " denoted any music played in a room or chamber, and not as it now does, music in which each part is played by only one performer. The 18th century symphony *was* chamber music; it was not designed to be played by swollen orchestras in vast halls to audiences numbered by the thousand.

* * *

In the appended list (Appendix A) will be found the names of most of the composers of symphonies or overtures in the 18th century, together with the number of such works by each that are known to survive in print.[2] Any attempt to enumerate the MS. works would have been doomed to failure, for the MS. copies are far too widely scattered and often inaccessible, also because there can be no doubt that very many have been lost or destroyed. Even so, the numbers given are far short of the true figures, as it is impossible to suppose that some composers of symphonies have not escaped the writer's notice, or that some of the printed works have not been missed or overlooked. Although the total figure is impressive, it could certainly be greatly increased if systematic search were made in all the world's libraries, private collections and unknown repositories of old and forgotten music.

In Appendix B will be found the names of some composers (names encountered more or less by chance) who wrote symphonies and overtures, but of whose output the writer has been unable to trace any printed copies.

If one could add to the number of known printed works the incalculable number of MS. works, the total figure would be much greater and would probably run into the thousands.

---

[1] Cucuel, *Études sur un Orchestre au XVIIIme siècle*, p. 14.
[2] The numbers include some *Symphonies Concertantes*, but not the Trio-Symphonies, of which a great many were published.

And what it all added up to was the handful of symphonies by Haydn and Mozart that are now so often heard in our concert-rooms.

How many symphonies did it take to make one good one? If an answer could be given, it would have to be in hundreds. It was a big price to pay, but it was well worth it.

Appendix A

Composers of symphonies or overtures published in the 18th century

Composer	published works
ABEL, C. F., 1725–1787 ..	.. 37
ALESSANDRI, F., 1747–1798 ..	6
ARNE, T. A., 1710–1778	.. 15
ARNOLD, S., 1740–1802 ..	.. 6
BACH, C. P. E., 1714–1788	.. 5
BACH, J. C., 1735–1782 ..	.. 37
BALDAN, A.	.. 6
BARRIÈRE, E. B. J., b.1749	.. 1
BARSANTI, F., c.1690–c.1760 ..	9
BARTHÉLEMON, F. H., 1741–1808	.. 6
BECK, F., 1730–1809 ..	.. 25
BEECKE, I. von, 1733–1803	.. 12
BERNASCONI, A., 1706–1784 ..	1
BIANCHI, F., 1752–1810 ..	.. 1
BLAINVILLE, C. H., 1711–1769(?)	2
BLOIS, de[1]	4
BOCCHERINI, L., 1743–1805	.. 22
BODE, J. J. C., 1730–1793	.. 6
BONONCINI, G. B., b.1672	.. 6
BORGHI, L., d.1806 ..	.. 6
BOYCE, W., 1710–1779 ..	.. 12
BURANELLI (Galuppi ?)..	.. 1
CAMBINI, G. G., 1746–1825	.. 35
CAMERLOHER, P. von, 1718–1782	.. 18
CANNABICH, Chas., 1769–1806	2
CANNABICH, Chris., 1731–1798	27
CHALON, C.	.. 6
CHARTRAIN, d.1793 ..	.. 8
CIAMPI, L. V.(?), b. 1719	.. 6
CLEMENTI, M., 1752–1832	.. 2
COLLET, R. or J.(?) ..	.. 6
CRISPI, P., 1737–1797 ..	.. 1
DESAIDES (Dezède) N., c.1740–1792	.. 1
DITTERSDORF, C. von, 1739–1799	.. 33
EBERL, A., 1766–1807 ..	.. 1
EDELMANN, J. F., 1749–1794 ..	1
EICHNER, E., 1740–1777 ..	.. 27
ESSER, C. M., c.1736– ..	.. 12
FILTZ, A., 1726–1760 ..	.. 18[2]

Composer	published works
FIORILLO, F., b.1753 ..	.. 5
FISCHER, F., 1723–1805 ..	.. 6
FÖRSTER, C., 1693–1745 ..	6
FRÄNZL, I., 1736–1811 ..	.. 3
FREDERICK the GREAT	.. 1
FRITZ, G., 1716–1782 ..	.. 6
GALUPPI, B., 1706–1785	.. 12
GIARDINI, F. de, 1716–1796	.. 7
GLASER, J. M., b.1725 ..	.. 6
GLUCK, C. W., 1714–1787	.. 6
GOSSEC, F. J., 1734–1829	.. 45
GRAF, C. E., c.1726–1804	.. 42
GRAUN, J. G., 1698–1771	.. 2
GRAUN, C. H., 1701–1759	.. 2
GREEN, M., 1695–1755 ..	.. 6
GREINER, J. T., c.1750–	.. 13
GRÉTRY, A. E. M., 1741–1813 ..	9
GUÉNIN, M. A., 1744–1819	.. 14
GYROWETZ, A., 1763–1850	.. 26
HANDEL, G. F., 1685–1759	.. 66[a]
HASSE, J. A., 1699–1783 ..	.. 6
HAYDEN, G.(?)	.. 1
HAYDN, F. J., 1732–1809	.. 59[4]
HAYDN, J. M., 1737–1806	.. 4
HEINSIUS, E.	.. 6
HERSCHEL, F. W., 1738–1822 ..	1
HERSCHEL, J., c.1734–1792 ..	2
HERTEL, J. W., 1727–1789	.. 12
HIMMEL, F. H., 1765–1814	.. 2
HODERMANN, G. C. ..	.. 2
HOFFMEISTER, F. A., 1754–1812	6
HOLZBAUER, I., 1711–1783	.. 30
HOOK, J., 1746–1827 ..	.. 1
HUPFELD, B., 1717–1794	.. 12
JOMMELLI, N., 1714–1774	.. 4
JUST, J. A., c.1750(?)–c.1800	.. 7
KAMMELL, A., c.1740–c.1788 ..	6
KELLY, 6th Earl of, 1732–1781 ..	15
KLÖFFLER, J. F., d.1792	.. 6
KOSPOTH, O. C. E. von, 1750–1817	.. 3
KOTZWARA, F., d.1791 ..	.. 2
KOZELUCH, L. A., 1754–1818 ..	9

1. Pseudonym of Chas. Giu. Xavier van Gronnenrade.
2. Probably many more.
3. Overtures.
4. 53 Sym. 6 Over., omitting many spurious and doubtful works.

Appendix A—Continued

Composer	published works
KRAFT, F. ...	6
KREUSSER, G. A., 1743–1811	23
KROMMER, F., 1760–1831	5
KÜCHLER, J.	2
KUNZEN, F. L., 1761–1817	2
LACHNITH, L. W., 1746–1820	15
LANG, J. G., 1724–1794(?)	6
LANGLE, H. F. M., 1741–1807	1
LEDUC, S., c.1748–1777	7
LINLEY, T., Jun., 1756–1778	1
LUCCHESI, A., 1741–c.1800	3
MALDERE, P. van, 1729–1768	24
MARSH, J., 1752–1828	13
MARTINI, G. St., c.1693–c.1750	8
MARTINI, G. B., 1701–1775	24
MARTINI (il Tedesco), 1741–1816	3
MASCH	1
MEDER, J. G.	12
MIROGLIO, P. J.,	6
MONSIGNY, P. A., 1729–1817	1
MOULINGHEN, L. C., b.1753	6
MOULINGHEN, J. B., b.1751	1
MOZART, W. A., 1756–1791	14
MYSLIWECEK, J., 1737–1781	14
NAUMANN, J. G., 1741–1801	2
NICOLAY, V., d.c.1798–1799	6
NORRIS, T., 1741–1790	6
PAISIELLO, G., 1741–1816	1
PASQUALI, N., d.1757	12
PEPUSCH, J. C., 1667–1752	1
PEREZ, D.(?), 1711–1778	1
PFEIFFER, J. M.	1
PHILIDOR (Danican) F. A., 1726–1795	1
PICCINI, N., 1728–1800	4
PICHL, W., 1741–1805	28
PLEYEL, I. J., 1757–1831	34
PUGNANI, G., 1731–1798	13
PUHL, W.	6
RAIMONDI, I., c.1735–1813	2
REICHA, J., 1746–1795	7
REICHARDT, J. F., 1752–1814	7
RICCI, P.(?), c.1733–	12
RICHTER, F. X., 1709–1789	33
ROMBERG, A. J., 1767–1821	9
ROSETTI (Röszler) F. A., 1750–1792	19
RUGGI, F.(?)	7
RULOFF, B., c.1737–1801	3
RUST, F. W., 1739–1796	1
SACCHINI, A. M. G., 1734–1786	1
ST. GEORGE, le Chevalier de, 1745–1799	6
SAMMARTINI, See MARTINI	
SAMPIERI, N.	3
SAXONY, Princess Royal of (Maria Antonia)	1
SCHENKER	6
SCHMITT, J., d.1808	11
SCHMITTBAUER, J. A., 1718–1809	4
SCHOBERT, J., c.1720–1767	6
SCHUSTER, J., 1748–1812	1
SCHWINDL, F., d.1786	24
SIEVERS, J. F. L., c.1740–1806	1
SMETHERGELL, W.	12
SMITH, J. C., 1712–1795	1
SPANGENBURG, G. C.	1
STAMITZ, J. W. A., 1717–1757	39
STAMITZ, C., 1746–1801	45
STUMPF, J. C., d.1801	6
TELEMANN, G. P., 1681–1767	7
TOESCHI, C. G., 1724–1788	37
TOESCHI, J. B., d.1800	18
VALENTINI, Giov., d.1791(?)	9
VALENTINI, Gius., b.1680	12
VANHALL, J. B., 1739–1813	12
VEICHTNER, F. A., c.1745–	6
WAGENSEIL, G. C., 1715–1777	13
WISEMANN	1
WITZTHUMB, I., 1723–1816	1
WRANITZKI, P., 1756–1808	27
ZEBRO, M. G.	1
ZINCK, B. F., 1743–1801	1
ZINGONI, G. B.	8
Total	**1,643**

Appendix B

Some composers of unpublished symphonies or overtures

ADAM, J., d.1784
ASPELMAYER, F., 1721–1786
BABBI, C., 1748–1814
BACH, Jos.
BACH, W. F., 1710–1784
BENDA, F., 1709–1786
BENDA, G. (J. A.), 1722–1795
BINDER, C. S., 1724–1789
FORKEL, J. N., 1749–1818
GASSMANN, F. L., 1729–1774
GEBEL, G., 1709–1753
GRAUPNER, C., 1683–1760 (116 Sym. 80 Over.)
HARRER, G., 1703–1755
HENNIG, C. F.
HERTEL, J. C., 1699–1754 (over 100 Sym.)
HILLER, J. A., 1728–1804 (30 Sym.)
HOFFMANN, L., c.1730–1793
HOECKH, C., 1707–1772
HURLEBUSCH, K. F., 1696–1765
JANITSCH, Anton, 1753–1812
KIRNBERGER, J. P., 1721–1783
KOHAUT, F. or J. (?)
KRUMPHOLZ, J. B., c.1745–1790
KUNZEN, A. C., 1720–1781
KUNZEN, J. P., 1696–1757

MANN, J. C., 1726–1782
MARPURG, F. W., 1718–1795
MASCHEK, V., 1755–1831
MOLTER, J. M., d.1765 (169 Sym.)
MONN, G. M., 1717–1750
MOZART, Leopold, 1719–1787
ORDONNEZ, C. de 1739–1786
ORSLER (Orschler) J. G., 1698–1766
PISENDEL, G. J., 1687–1755
REUTTER, J. A. K. G., 1708–1772
RIEDT, F. W., 1712–1784
RIEPEL, J., 1708–1782
RIGEL, H. J., 1741–1799
ROLLE, J. H., 1718–1785
SCHAFFRATH, C., 1709–1763
SCHALE, C. F., 1713–1800
SCHEIBE, J. A., 1708–1776
SCHÜRER, A., d.c.1780
SPERGER, J. M., d.1812
STAMITZ, Anton, 1754–1820
STARZER, J., 1726–1787
TISCHER, J. N., b.1707
TZARTH (Czarth) G., 1708–1778
WEBER, F. A., 1753–1806
WERNER, G. J., 1695–1766
WIEDNER, J. K., c.1724–1774
ZACH, J., 1699–1773

INDEX

ABEL, 21, 23, 26, 36, 37, 43, 55, 66
ARNE, 10, 11, 12, 17, 29, 31, 34, 37, 46, 51, 57
BACH, J. C., 11, 12, 21, 23, 26, 35, 36, 38, 54
BACH, J. S., 9, 29, 30
BECK, 19
BEETHOVEN, 16, 21, 26, 45
BOCCHERINI, 24, 26, 36
CANNABICH, 19, 36, 38
CIMAROSA, 58
CODA, 35, 36, 39
CRAMER, 27
DEVELOPMENT, 35, 68
DITTERSDORF, 3, 24, 26, 27, 36, 42, 56, 61
EICHNER, 36
EXPOSITION, 34
FASCH, 9
FILTZ, 12, 19, 35, 52
FORM, 7, 28
FORSTER, 9
FRANZL, 19
GOSSEC, 12, 19, 27, 35, 52
GRAUN, 9
GRETRY, 58
HANDEL, 9, 12, 15, 29, 31, 46, 57
HASSE, 9
HAYDN, 1, 4, 16, 20, 22, 23, 25, 26, 31, 38, 39, 43, 44, 61, 62, 65
HOLZBAUER, 19, 27, 30, 35, 53, 61
JOMMELLI, 12, 38
KEISER, 9
KOZELUCH, 26
LINLEY, 12, 36, 58
LULLI, 9, 29
MALDERE, P. van, 20, 35, 53
MANNHEIM, 18, 19, 26, 37
MEHUL, 27
MINUET, 9, 13, 24, 29, 30, 31, 37
MONN, 19, 37
MOZART, 1, 4, 16, 20, 21, 23, 24, 26, 31, 38, 43, 60, 62

MYSLIWECEK, 27
NICOLAY, 37
ORCHESTRAL PARTS, 1, 5, 15, 41, 44, 69
ORCHESTRATION, 45-50
OUVERTURE (French), 8-10, 13, 16, 28, 40
PASQUALI, 17
PHILIDOR, 58
PICCINI, 12
PICHL, 27, 36
PLEYEL, 26, 44, 45, 56
POUPLINIERE, La, 20, 70
PUGNANI, 12, 26
PURCELL, 10, 29
QUANTZ, 10, 28, 29
RAIMONDI, 27
RAMEAU, 10
REUTTER, 19, 37
RICHTER, 19, 36
RONDO, 38, 39
ROSETTI, 27, 36
SACCHINI, 12
SAMMARTINI (St. Martini), 16
SCARLATTI, 10, 11
SCHMITTBAUER, 36
SCHNEIDER, 9
SCHURMANN, 9
SCHWINDL, 23, 31, 36, 55
SCORE, 40, 44, 45
SECOND SUBJECT, 32, 34
SEMI-SONATA FORM, 35
SINFONIA (Italian), 8, 10-13, 16
SONATA FORM, 10, 11, 13, 17, 20, 32, 36
STAMITZ, C., 19, 27, 36
STAMITZ, J., 6, 18, 20, 22, 26, 30, 35, 44, 47, 51
TELEMANN, 9
TOESCHI, 19, 30, 35, 54
TZARTH, 19
VANHALL, 3, 36
WAGENSEIL, 19, 37